THE
BLESSINGS
OF
LIBERTY

THE
BLESSINGS
OF
LIBERTY

———— * ————

By FRANCIS PICKENS MILLER

———— * ————

CHAPEL HILL
THE UNIVERSITY OF
NORTH CAROLINA
PRESS

1936

Copyright, 1936, by
THE UNIVERSITY OF NORTH CAROLINA PRESS

TO
HELEN HILL
WHOSE SHARE IN THIS BOOK

IS TOO GREAT

TO BE MENTIONED

FOREWORD

———————— * ————————

THE REVIVAL OF THOUGHT ON PUBLIC AFFAIRS IS A nation-wide phenomenon. Certain trends of thought are in the air. It would be an endless and pointless undertaking to enumerate how much or in what way I have been influenced by this or that opinion or this or that publication. The reader of current literature on public affairs will recognize the extent of my debt to the research and thought of others. That debt is the measure of my gratitude.

CONTENTS

Foreword　vii

I. Liberty as Security and Freedom in Balance　1

II. Weights in the Balance between Freedom and Security　12

III. What is Freedom?　17

IV. What is Security?　31

V. Can the Union be Preserved?　46

VI. Can Democracy Function on a Continental Scale?　58

VII. Liberty Under the New Deal　70

VIII. A Bill of Particulars　93

THE
BLESSINGS
OF
LIBERTY

*

"We, the people of the United States, in order to... secure the blessings of liberty to ourselves and our posterity, do ordain and establish this constitution for the United States of America."

Preamble to the Constitution of 1787

*

"...no free government, or the blessing of liberty, can be preserved to any people but by... frequent recurrence to fundamental principles."

George Mason of Gunston Hall

CHAPTER
ONE

———— * ————

LIBERTY AS SECURITY AND FREEDOM IN BALANCE

THE CIRCUMSTANCES OF OUR NATIONAL LIFE REQUIRE that citizens once more define the *ends* of society. American society was founded to secure specific ends. During the course of one hundred and fifty years these ends tended to become increasingly obscured as they became increasingly taken for granted. They were sentimentally assumed and practically ignored. Because ignored they were gradually supplanted. The purposes by which men lived came to differ from and then to conflict with the purposes which originally dominated the republic. The experiences of the past seven years have made it obvious that the maintenance of democratic institutions depends upon the reassertion of democratic ends and their definition in terms of the actualities of contemporary life.

The necessity laid upon Americans to redefine the ends of their society is a necessity derived in part from the crisis of political and economic institutions through which we are passing. But while the prolongation of the crisis may accentuate the urgency of definition, the crisis itself should not be thought of as the sole or as even the most important reason for attempting a definition.

The health of human nature depends upon the continual rediscovery and reaffirmation of high social objectives. The good life is synonymous with the conscious establishment of good "ends." If men cease their efforts to translate the meaning of these "ends" into forms appropriate to changing actualities they will soon cease to be men. In the human sphere to be merely repetitive is to die.

The final definition of human ends can only be given in terms of philosophy or theology. Neither politics nor economics, neither sociology nor technology can supply the material for giving a conclusive answer to the question "What is the chief end of man?" They cannot because man is a reality more inclusive than the very segmentary bits of reality with which these various branches of knowledge have to do. Man in the essence of his being is super-economic and super-technological. But he cannot prove this by affirming it. Nor can he prove it by ignoring or belittling economic and technological realities.

Man can prove his super-economic destiny only by demonstrating his mastery of the economic forces which he has himself evoked. He can prove that he is of more value than the industrial machine only by organizing the mechanical forces of production in such a way that they will serve rather than thwart human ends.

What are the great ends of American society? A century and a half ago men thought they could give an answer to this question. They wrote in the preamble to the Constitution of 1787:

> We, the People of the United States, in order to form a more perfect union, establish justice, insure domestic tranquillity, provide for the common defence, promote the general welfare, and *secure the Blessings of Liberty* to ourselves and our Posterity, do ordain and establish this constitution for the United States of America.

This description of the ends of American society has never been equaled in its simplicity, conciseness, and dignity. Of all the great phrases used in the preamble the phrase "We the People of the United States, in order to ... secure the Blessings of Liberty to ourselves and our Posterity, do ordain and establish this constitution for the United States of America" is perhaps nearest the heart of our most authentic American tradition. The hunger for liberty, the will to secure liberty, runs in an unbroken thread through our history from the landing of the first settlers. Our greatest wars have been fought in its name—to secure liberty for ourselves or others. And it remains the supreme objective of American society. Yet when the Hoover-Republicans and the Smith-Democrats say they want liberty it is obvious that what they want has little in common with what the Progressives or the

New Deal-Democrats also want in the name of liberty. This lack of thought and this confusion of thought is a reflection of the chaos in the soul of the nation itself—a chaos which will eventually produce national disintegration unless the nation can achieve a new unity through acquiring a new sense of direction.

In spite of the fact that the same word is used to describe diametrically opposite objectives, the appeal to liberty continues to be the most powerful appeal that can be addressed to the American people. It is consequently the duty of every citizen to do what he can to help clarify the meaning of liberty for American society at the present time. The object of this paper is to contribute to the process of clarification.

What is liberty? It is submitted that liberty is the condition in which all citizens enjoy both freedom and security and in which there is the most perfect balance between freedom and security. It is further submitted that the creation and preservation of the conditions in which it is possible for citizens to exercise their freedom and enjoy their security, and the maintenance of the balance between freedom and security is the first obligation of government.

When can citizens exercise their freedom? Citizens can exercise their freedom when they can believe what they will, say what they want, and meet to promote their common interests. But if men have no work or property or wages or food, the exercise of their freedom to believe, to speak, and to assemble is

Security and Freedom

of no use to them. To remind starving men that they are free is mockery. If freedom is to be enjoyed it is obvious that certain specific economic conditions for its enjoyment must first be fulfilled.

When can citizens enjoy security? Citizens can enjoy security when each has a consuming power sufficient to provide a decent standard of living. But if men have no freedom, well-fed bodies will be small consolation for starved minds and shriveled spirits.

The good life requires freedom and security. When both are united in the same society the citizens of that society may be said to enjoy liberty.

If this is a correct definition of liberty it follows that liberty is not the same thing as freedom. On the contrary it is much more inclusive than freedom. A man may be free and yet because of economic insecurity be unable to enjoy liberty. In other words liberty is a compound composed of economic goods as well as civil rights.

But it also follows that neither is liberty the same thing as security. A man may possess a fair share of this world's goods and yet be unable to enjoy liberty because he is not allowed to speak his mind on public affairs or take common action with his fellows.

If the blessings of liberty are to be secured for us in the United States we must aim at the possession of a measure of both freedom and security. The balance between them is all-important. Exaggerated and perverted freedom is certain to create insecurity, while a perverted and exaggerated security is sure to destroy freedom. We must achieve the kind of freedom that is compatible with security and the kind of security that is compatible with freedom.

But the character of history is such that a perfect balance between freedom and security can seldom be achieved, or if once achieved can rarely be maintained except over brief periods. The inventive and dynamic spirit of man is constantly releasing new types of social forces which destroy the balance by overweighting one side or the other. It then becomes the task of citizens who are aware of their responsibility to restore the balance by becoming champions of the underweighted side.

During some periods in the evolution of society it will be more important to advocate freedom than security. During others it will be more important to advocate security than freedom. The primary need of the latter half of the eighteenth century was for more freedom. The primary need of the first half of the twentieth century is for more security.

But neither one of these two great objectives of human society can long survive without the other. If personal freedom disappears personal security will shortly not be worth having. And if insecurity increases freedom will in turn lose its meaning. Hence in an age like our own, dominated by the fear of insecurity, the battle for security is the same thing as the battle for freedom. But it is essential to recognize in any given period which objective should have priority. For freedom and security seldom require equal emphasis. The out-of-balance character of national life usually means that government has to be preoccupied with either the task of restoring freedom or the task of restoring security. And the assignment of priority in legislative councils is extremely important. Policy founded on a wrong estimate of priority may be more disastrous than no policy at all.

It is of course true that the champions of whichever side is out-of-balance are apt in a period of national crisis to assert the exclusive claims of one particular emphasis with such partisan ardor that essential balancing factors will be jeopardized or even destroyed. The zeal for liberty may result in chaos and the zeal for security may produce oppression unless the authority of the one is constantly corrected by the authority of the other. But as long as some measure of balance is preserved between them, the wise statesman can steer a course which will save the people from either excessive want resulting in revolution, or excessive regulation resulting in tyranny.

The Declaration of Independence and the Federal Constitution were attempts to achieve and maintain a more perfect balance between security and freedom in the out-of-balance circumstances of colonial life. If we are to be as successful as our forefathers of the eighteenth century in restoring the lost balance of American life, it is essential to recognize the contrast between present-day society and the society of colonial times. The men of the Revolution were citizens of a dynamic society with a rapidly expanding frontier. The expanding frontier has gone. We are citizens of an enclosed society in which the task of consolidation is far more important than the task of expansion. Like an army on the offensive we have gone so far beyond our original objectives that we are in danger of losing everything unless we stop and dig in and consolidate the area behind us.

The society of the expanding frontier achieved a balance between security and freedom through devotion to the virtues of individual initiative. The digging-in society of today can only achieve similar balance through devotion to the virtues required for persons who live in responsible relationship to other persons.

In our age of pioneer expansion men won their economic security by individual exercise of freedom to exploit nature, with its fatal sequence of freedom-license-insecurity and the end of liberty. In our age of consolidation men can only rewin their personal liberty by creating personal security through collective social action.

A democratic society is one in which the citizens have the power to choose and remove their governors with a view to maintaining a proper balance between security and freedom. The Constitution of 1787 guaranteed to the citizens the exercise of this power and provided a framework within which their will could be made effective. The framework erected by the Constitution was neither narrow nor inflexible. On the contrary it was both spacious and flexible.

spacious enough to accommodate the increments of a changing social order, and flexible enough to permit adjustments essential to the restoration of balance between freedom and security.

The Constitution, however, is not so flexible and hospitable that any and every kind of social system can find room for free expression within the society which it describes. The Constitution implies very definite limits beyond which certain social forces cannot go. It implies, for example, the use of the democratic process as the means of obtaining necessary social change. But the democratic process cannot be used if there is widespread economic insecurity. The Constitution, therefore, serves as a permanent mandate for citizens to concern themselves with the positive task of creating social and economic conditions essential to the survival of democratic institutions.

The Constitution itself does not decree the form which social and economic forces shall take in any age. It merely defines the frontiers within which they shall operate. But that definition is in itself a command to each succeeding generation to recognize the realities of its own time, to understand the conditions which have to be fulfilled in each age if democratic institutions are to survive, and to see to it that the fulfillment of those conditions becomes national policy.

American statesmen of the latter half of the eighteenth century could not foresee the character of the new economic and social forces which were to evolve during the next century. They could not know that the freedom guaranteed by the Constitution would be taken advantage of to release new social forces which would in time threaten the very foundation of liberty itself.

The circumstances of the nineteenth century glorified the acquisitive as compared with the coöperative instincts. The lure of settling a vast, rich, unoccupied continent produced the myth of stalwart individualism while new industrial processes accentuated the concentration of economic and financial power in fewer and fewer hands. As a result the clever and ruthless took what they could get, and the taking was very good, while the mass of the people took what was left, which was not very much. Meanwhile the courts said in effect that this was the kind of society anticipated by the Constitution, thus effectively vetoing preventive measures which might have been taken.

The consequence was an emerging duality in American life. Side by side with democratic political institutions grew up autocratic economic institutions. The potential disruptive force of this inner contradiction is no less terrible than was the disruptive force of the contradiction between slave states and free states. If a house divided against itself could not stand then it cannot stand now. Both types of institutions cannot permanently survive within the same society. Their ultimate purposes are too divergent to be reconciled. One will eventually be eliminated by the other. For some years the drift has been towards the elimination of democratic political institutions by autocratic economic forces. Since 1933 that drift has been momentarily arrested. But the present is merely an interlude.

The issue remains, and a realist will hesitate to prophesy what the outcome will be. For the autocrats of industry and finance are the most powerful single group in the modern world. To maintain democratic institutions in the face of their pressure will require a citizenship informed and prepared to act intelligently and resolutely. There is still an interval when education and preparation is possible. But the time is short.

Either economic forces must be made subservient to democratic ends, or political institutions, and hence the whole of American life will in time be ruled by an oligarchy of industry and finance allied with the discontented propertyless classes. Can the economic forces of America be made to serve democratic ends instead of opposing them? Can these forces be made to secure the blessings of liberty instead of threatening to destroy them? Upon the solution of this problem the future of democratic institutions depends—not only in America but throughout the world, for the crisis of democracy is not an American crisis; it is a world crisis.

CHAPTER TWO

---- * ----

WEIGHTS IN THE BALANCE BETWEEN FREEDOM AND SECURITY

Exercise of initiative by citizens, groups of citizens, and subdivisions of government is a basic assumption of government in a country which enjoys liberty. The problem of such a government differs in kind from the problem of government in a totalitarian state.

The problem of a totalitarian government is to put into effect a single, centrally formulated program, under the direct charge of a unified executive. Such a government assumes initiative in its subjects only in respect to administration, labor, and obedience. Its only limits are the limits of the tolerable, limits pushed ever farther into the distance by the combined action of uncontradicted propaganda and irresponsible force.

The problem of government in a democracy is fundamentally different. It is primarily a problem of co-ordinating the independently vital objectives of the regions, groups, and individuals under its jurisdiction in such a way as to secure the blessings of liberty to its citizens.

The purpose of that coördination is not merely to sanction the resultant of existing forces. The government has itself an objective, a long-term general purpose, declared in its Constitution and amplified in the customs of its national life. The Administration in power at any given time, furthermore, has specific objectives, advanced by the victorious political party as immediate expressions of the long-term purposes of the Constitution.

The problem of today's American government is therefore to coördinate, in the interest of liberty, the forces whose actions, if unrelated to each other, would limit or destroy either the freedom or the security of parts or all of the citizenry.

The establishment of government on a continental scale was a feat of blind daring. Its maintenance requires clearsighted realism and administrative skill of a superior order. The variety of interests now included within the jurisdiction of the United States presents the government with a problem of unsurpassed magnitude.

Basic to the maintenance of a sound governmental structure is recognition of the pine-to-palm, dogwood-to-redwood differences between the regions forming these United States, for out of the climatic and geographic variations from which they spring, spring also sectional differences which have once threatened to

Balkanize the continent and may well do so again.

The civilization of the sections has produced both social myths and social facts, with each of which (and the two are often in conflict) the national government must be concerned. Take two examples. Take the social myth of the West: the great open spaces where men are men, where security is the reward of individual effort, where freedom is unrestrained. Take the social fact of the West of these last drought years: a land salvaged from sun and wind by the collective resources of the nation, contributing more families than any other area to the nation's transient relief population that seeks to pick up a precarious livelihood on the road. Take the social myth of the South: moonlight and jasmine, pride and gentle living, a sense of obligation to look after its people. Take the social fact of the South: squalor, illiteracy, the major breeding place of the nation's population.

Overlapping the differences in geography are the differences in ages between the societies of the sections. The East was a functioning society when the Mississippi and all its tributaries ran through a silent wilderness. During the period of its consolidation, the nineteenth century Middle West perforce looked to the East for credit and for manufactured goods; the attitude of the twentieth century Middle West continues to express the alternate dependence and defiance of the colonial mind.

For three generations the attitude of the post-civil-war South toward the North has been that of a conquered territory toward its conqueror; in recent years the exploitation of southern resources by northern corporations has superimposed upon this feeling the characteristic colonial pattern.

Maintenance of government on a continental scale requires accommodation of these attitudes in a mutual sense of common direction. Nor are separate locations in time and space the only distances which the bridges of continental union must be built to span.

Given our national history and our national temper, it is possible—it has already happened once—for sectional ways of living to move too far apart for the bridges of continental union to sustain traffic between them. It is equally possible—and the question of imminence may not be remote—for standards of living in the country to move too far apart for a single constitution to find support on such widely separated levels. Government maintained on a continental scale must concern itself with differences in wealth.

In the United States at present the range of income is wide as between individuals, as between states, as between regions. It is wide as between the industrial and the agricultural sectors of the American economy; it is wide as between individuals engaged in each sector. During the period of preëmption of the continent, citizens of the United States made these differences in wealth off the country; in more recent years they have made them off each other.

Because of these divergent movements, national unity is under strain. A government which maintains liberty in the United States must coördinate within its legal and administrative framework the dynamic forces which make American life, including the forces which these differences express. They are dynamic forces; their initiative is properly beyond the state's control. Their actions, however, are properly subject to control by the government insofar as they affect the liberty of its citizens, insofar as they affect that balance between freedom and security without which democracy cannot long endure.

CHAPTER
THREE

———— * ————

WHAT IS
FREEDOM?

THE THESIS OF THIS PAMPHLET IS THAT FREEDOM AND security in balance mean liberty, and that the first obligation of government is to assure a society in which freedom and security can be equally enjoyed.

Everyone admits that the ideal of freedom is the bed-rock of the American highway. What do we mean by freedom? What kind of freedom is it that, existing in balance with security, equates liberty? In what sense should the word freedom be used by believers in democratic institutions?

The fact that there are no commonly accepted answers to these questions accounts to a considerable extent for the economic waste that accompanies our ill-considered and half-baked experiments in national policy, together with the disillusion which the failure of these experiments inevitably breeds. We cannot expect less waste and more effectiveness in our experiments until the body of citizens begins to acquire a sense of direction, and a sense of what freedom means and what steps have to be taken to achieve it.

An emotional sense of movement can be artificially stimulated without any sense of direction. That is the state in which most of us are living in 1936. It is a thrilling experience and a very dangerous one. Under the false impression that going places is sure to land us at the right place we have confused acceleration with direction. If we are to arrive at the right place we must in all sanity know where we want to go. Clarity of concept is a necessary prelude to a clear sense of direction.

What is this freedom that is the bed-rock of the American way?

Next to the desire for food, the desire for freedom seems to have been the deepest and most consistent hunger of mankind. Most of the great movements of history are associated with the desire for freedom.

Because of the circumstances of early American life, freedom was thought of very largely in negative terms. The result was a distortion of its true meaning. For it is the essence of freedom to be positive as well as negative. Freedom *from* something has no meaning unless it is also freedom *for* something.

Among our ancestors of the eighteenth century the "for" was so obvious that it could be taken for granted. They desired freedom to enter and possess the Promised Land which was the North American continent. But they wanted to do this in their own

What Is Freedom?

way, and they finally realized that they could not do it in their own way as long at they were ruled from London. The freedom for which they fought, therefore, was freedom *from* overseas control. Our Protestant tradition had in any case disposed us to associate freedom with negation. The fact that the nation itself was born of rebellion served to confirm this disposition as a permanent trait of our national character.

The negative aspect of freedom thus became dominant, but even during the War of Independence it was by no means entirely dominant. The question "freedom for what" could not be avoided so long as a new society had to be established. The theory of natural rights provided material for the first attempt at an answer. It was asserted that "men are endowed by their Creator with certain unalienable Rights, that among these are Life, Liberty, and the pursuit of Happiness.—That to secure these rights Governments are instituted among men." The preamble to the Constitution provided a second great answer to the query "freedom for what." The bill of rights embodied in the first ten amendments to the Constitution presented a third. These answers were necessarily given in very general terms. But the general terms employed described aims and objectives which seemed far more concrete to the men of that time than they seem to us today.

It is our business to put concrete content into these terms in the light of the actualities of our own time.

Freedom in 1936 means both "freedom for" and "freedom from" just as it did in 1776.

In 1776 men desired "freedom from" because the conditions of life had come to seem intolerable. The form of government under which they lived appeared destructive to life, liberty, and the pursuit of happiness. They therefore resolved to institute new government.

In the nineteen-thirties there is once more a rising tide of desire to escape from conditions which have proved increasingly intolerable. These mass movements of hope and fear constitute the stuff out of which the great changes of history are made. They are not the product of the demagogue's magic. They spring from economic and cultural actualities. If these actualities are faced and dealt with the social order can be changed and possibly improved. If, on the other hand, these actualities are ignored or repressed, the rising tide of discontent will finally turn into a tidal wave which will sweep all before it.

Superficial appearances during the summer of 1936 may seem to indicate that conditions that threatened to become intolerable have at least been greatly alleviated if they have not been entirely removed. Was not the national income produced in 1935 up $13,400,-000,000, or 34 per cent, above the national income produced in 1932? Was not the proportion of national income paid out for salaries, wages and other labor payments in 1935 the greatest on record? Did not the index numbers of farm prices rise from 65 per cent

WHAT IS FREEDOM?

of the prewar average in 1932 to 108 per cent in 1935? Has not prosperity returned with the New Deal? Is not everyone free again to pursue happiness? Has not the President told us that the worst enemy of all, fear itself, has been removed?

Superficial appearances were never more deceptive. The fact remains that over half of the farmers in the country, and in some states two-thirds of the farmers, still do not own the soil they till. The fact remains that while industrial production, in May, 1936, stood at 94.3 per cent of the 1924-29 average, total factory payrolls stood at only 76.8 per cent, and payrolls per employed wage earner at only 89.5 per cent of their averages for the same years. The fact remains that though employment has increased by some three million since 1933, the unemployment figure remains about the same because of the natural increase in population. The fact remains that the ghost of fear has been only temporarily banished through relief expenditure on a scale which cannot be continued without the eventual collapse of national credit. The fact remains that the major problems which confronted the nation in 1933 still confront the nation. The New Deal has not yet solved one of them. These are the actualities of the situation.

In other words, conditions persist which an increasing number of citizens can only regard as intolerable. This explains why the coal miners will not tranquilly accept reversion to the previous state of affairs even though the Supreme Court has thrown out the Guffey

Coal Act. This explains why the lines are being drawn for a titanic struggle between labor and capital in the steel industry. This explains why there are signs everywhere of increasing industrial conflict. This explains the sinister rumblings even among the most powerless and degraded portions of our population—the sharecroppers of the Cotton Belt.

The existence of these conditions proves that there are forces operating in the United States which are destructive of life, liberty, and the pursuit of happiness. As long as these forces continue to operate those who feel their impact will desire freedom from them. In 1776 the forces of destruction seemed to be chiefly political. The formula of escape was simple, "new government." At present the forces of destruction are chiefly economic. Because of their complexity a sane and rational formula of escape is infinitely more difficult to discover. Under these circumstances an answer to the question *freedom for what* becomes doubly imperative.

Reduced to its simplest terms the answer is freedom to earn a decent American standard of living on the part of those who are now denied that freedom. The freedom to earn a decent living depends upon the existence of certain economic, legal, and social conditions. These conditions do not exist at present for large sections of the population. It is therefore the business of government to establish these conditions. As such conditions are established, it is the business of

WHAT IS FREEDOM? 23

citizens to earn by their individual and collective effort the living which these conditions allow.

It is an illusion to suppose that the State can guarantee a decent living to its citizens. If it attempts to do so the evils incurred will be greater than the benefits bestowed. A combination of conditions determined by government and voluntary efforts undertaken by citizens is the very essence of the American system. That is what differentiates it from societies in which the State destroys freedom in order to provide security.

Since the voluntary effort of citizens is as important as the determination of conditions by the State, "freedom for" must begin in 1936, as it did in 1776, with the assertion of personal rights. The liberties of free thought, free speech, free press and free assembly are as essential to self-government now as they ever were. Without these liberties voluntary social effort is impossible. Without them men lose through disuse those qualities which are most distinctly human and tend to revert to sub-human types. Culture cannot survive where these liberties have been destroyed. Men may retain their technical skill but if it is unrefined by cultural finesse the immense power which it puts at their disposal is more apt to be used for hellish than for humane purposes. This explains the rapid disintegration of European civilization in dictator-ruled countries.

The possession of these personal rights is an indispensable condition of creative social change. Their maintenance is therefore the first duty of the citizen.

It is particularly pertinent for our present purposes to remember that these basic rights guaranteed to all American citizens by the Constitution are strictly personal. They originate from within the individual. They are an expression of his own intrinsic nature. The citizen is free to exercise them as a man because he is a man and not because of any status he may have in society.

The corollary is that these rights are different in kind from such rights as property rights. Personal rights have nothing to do with rights over things or over other people. Nor does any external object regardless of its character or value endow an individual with such rights.

The all-important question then becomes, what is a person? The answer which the American business community has given to this question constitutes one of the most serious threats to freedom that has arisen in the past century and a half. The tendency to equate a man's life with his business life has rendered large groups of men incapable of distinguishing between the *persona realis* of the living human being and the *persona ficta* of the corporation. It is therefore not surprising that these men should claim for the shadowy business personalities in which they find their being and through which they control the country's wealth the liberties which are constitutionally guaranteed to living men.

The ascription to a corporation of personal rights

What Is Freedom?

gives that corporation *a right* over the minds and actions of its employees, in other words it is equivalent to the creation of a domestic despotism capable by a legal fiction of denying to living men in the name of the Constitution the very rights guaranteed to them by the Constitution. A situation is thus created which inevitably produces a "long train of abuses and usurpations" from which eventually men will inevitably revolt.

The preservation of freedom in the United States depends, therefore, upon the success of the courts in clearly distinguishing between the rights of persons and the rights of corporations.

It is obvious then that in the first instance "freedom for" means freedom to exercise civil liberties. But such freedom remains purely theoretical unless "freedom for" also means freedom to create the economic conditions without which liberty cannot be enjoyed. This is the crux of the problem as far as our time is concerned. It is the crux of the problem because for many years the trend of American life has been away from this kind of freedom. A larger and larger percentage of Americans has been unable to enjoy liberty since the means were not available to achieve a decent standard of living or even to maintain a semblance of economic independence.

Under such circumstances the power to create economic conditions favorable to freedom no longer resides among those who have already lost their freedom. The only power adequate to create these economic conditions is the power of the People as a whole acting through Government.

The Virginia Bill of Rights began with the declaration "that all men...have certain inherent natural rights, of which they cannot, by any compact, deprive or divest their posterity; among which are...the means of acquiring and possessing property." We might well choose this as the opening statement of our new charter of liberties.

According to the author of this declaration "the means of acquiring and possessing property" was a right of exactly the same kind as the right to life, liberty, and the pursuit of happiness.

For the purposes of the present argument the significance of this definition of natural rights is the distinction which is implied between "the means of acquiring and possessing property" and "the possession of property." The former is regarded as an absolute right. The use of the phrase "means of" is all important. It clearly indicates that "a right to *the means of* acquiring and possessing" is a different kind of right from what is now commonly called a property right or "the rights of property." In the Constitution-making period, the latter was obviously not thought of as an absolute right. The implication is that it is a relative right contingent upon the social good.

If this distinction is sound, the responsibility of government is clear. Where the means of acquiring and possessing property do not exist it is the function of government to create such conditions as may be neces-

WHAT IS FREEDOM?

sary for dispossessed citizens to have access to *the means*. Where individuals already possess property it is the function of government to see to it that they exercise their rights of possession in such a manner that others will not be deprived or divested of "the means of acquiring and possessing."

In the light of this distinction the responsibility of citizens also becomes equally clear. It is the duty of citizens to assert their absolute right to freedom of access to the means of acquiring and possessing property just as they assert their absolute right to freedom of speech, press, and assembly. It is furthermore the duty of citizens who possess property to recognize that freedom in the use of property is a very different thing from freedom of access to the means of acquiring it. The latter is good in itself. The former, namely the freedom contingent upon property rights, is, on the other hand, not good in itself. It is only good in relation to the use made of it.

Freedom derived from the possession of property is a positive good if its responsible use increases security throughout the community. Freedom derived from the possession of property is a positive evil if its responsible use decreases security throughout the community.

The labor policy employed by the Ford plant in Detroit when the shift was made from Model T to A exemplifies the irresponsible use of freedom. A large proportion of the 80,000 Ford employees live in Detroit. Mr. Ford lives out of Detroit and pays his local taxes in Dearborn and River Rouge. When the Ford plant was being reëquipped for the production of Model A the Ford employees were turned out on the street without unemployment insurance or any other provision for tiding over. The result was that the burden of supporting Mr. Ford's people fell directly on the taxpayers and relief agencies of the Detroit area. The middle classes provided through charity and taxation the funds which should have been a first charge upon the industry itself. This same phenomenon occurs with every temporary decrease of employment in the automobile industry, and the automobile industry and the City of Detroit are by no means exceptions to American industrial practice.

The use of freedom revealed in the foregoing analysis throws some light on the collapse of conservative leadership in America which is one of the most puzzling phenomena in the contemporary scene. The conservatives have the wealth, they have the power, and they have the education. Furthermore the United States is essentially a conservative country and would normally prefer to follow conservative leadership. During the nineteenth century the conservatives in England maintained their authority by sponsoring the great social reforms which characterized that period. Yet the conservatives in the United States lack sufficient authority to furnish a lead for either major party.

The collapse of conservative leadership is of course due to many different factors. Few conservatives of the American business world have behind them the kind of agrarian tradition which gives to many of their English cousins a sense of "noblesse oblige." Many economic and financial leaders in the United States, in spite of their great wealth and practical experience, are essentially illiterate as far as the problems of society and the affairs of State are concerned. But there are deeper reasons than these. American conservatives have forfeited their right to lead because they have misstated the problem of liberty and failed to understand that liberty is compounded as much of security as it is of freedom. They have limited their championship of liberty to "freedom from," and identified their own "freedom from" with the liberties of the Bill of Rights. They mistook property rights for personal rights and reserved these rights for those who already possessed them. In short, the conservatives have failed because they erroneously supposed that the freedom by which they had won their own security was equally available to men of ability in other sections of the population.

The classical expression of the American conservative mood was given in the autumn of 1935 by Mr. John W. Davis. During the course of an address to students he deplored the current interest in social security as unworthy of self-respecting men and added that the only group in this country that ever achieved perfect social security was the group of Negro slaves in the southern states prior to the Civil War. Grenville and Lord North probably made no remarks to George III that revealed more ignorance of what was happening in the American colonies than this remark reveals as to what is happening today in the American hinterland. It justifies the comment that there is another group in America which also enjoys the advantages which were the lot of Negro slaves before the Civil War and that is the group composed of those corporation lawyers who in return for rendering similar services to the industrial class enjoy similar security.

The reaction of the country to the Liberty League dinner represents a sound instinct. The mass of the people are intuitively aware that the declarations of these economic conservatives are unrelated to present circumstances. They are unrelated because they ignore the fact that the condition of liberty which they specify, namely the right to the means of acquiring and possessing property, is under present circumstances denied to vast sections of the population. The country will not trust conservative leadership again until the conservatives themselves give evidence of understanding more clearly the structure of the world in which they live and the nature of the forces with which government has to deal.

CHAPTER
FOUR

———— * ————

WHAT IS SECURITY?

SECURITY IS NOT A GOOD IN ITSELF. SLAVES HAVE BEEN secure. Subjects of tyrants have been secure, even as Party members are secure under today's dictatorships. But absence of security makes slaves of free men, and induces them to become subjects of tyrants.

Neither is security solely an economic good. Definition of security as economic security is subhuman. An animal that has food and shelter is secure; a man who has food and shelter and the requisite gadgets for an American standard of living but who lacks a religious and philosophic basis for his life is insecure. A decadent Protestantism and an adapted pragmatism have left us with wide areas of religious and philosophic insecurity, and part of our current difficulties are caused by our attempts to give religious and philosophic significance to concepts and criteria whose applicability is limited to the field of economic security.

The totalitarian state assumes the function of determining for its subjects the content of all sorts of security, religious, philosophical, economic. The democratic state bent on insuring liberty to its citizens provides the conditions within which the content of these various sorts of security can be individually—and by all individuals—sought.

Guarantee of religious liberty, of individual freedom to seek the salvation which is the religious symbol of security, is an indispensable function of a democratic government. But religious security is an inner and spiritual state, and while its presence or absence has a marked effect upon other aspects of the problem of security, its content is not affected by state action, and collective affirmation of its content is the function not of the state but of the church.

Economic security, on the other hand, is based upon external and material tangibles, to which the state is directly related through its system of law and administration. Economic security is derived from property, and property depends for its sanction upon the police, the legislature, and judiciary of the state.

A democracy that desires its citizens to be secure must face the fundamental question, what forms of property are conducive to liberty? How can the forces now directing the production and disposition of the nation's wealth be so related as to create conditions in which free men can enjoy liberty?

The security sought by today's American democracy is a special sort of security. It is not the security

WHAT IS SECURITY? 33

of *dependence*. It is the security of *interdependence*.

Its opposite, the insecurity of interdependence, is writ large in the recent history of America. Analysis of our current insecurity throws light on the task ahead.

For six years, the insecurity of interdependence has characterized the whole of our economic life; its agricultural sector has been distressed for nearer fifteen; the causes of both industrial and agricultural depression reach far back into the American past.

The pioneer in his clearing was a free man. He was also an anarchist. He was not the kind of an anarchist who seeks to destroy governmental order; he was an anarchist simply because no governmental order was there. He was independent for the excellent reason that there was nobody else around.

Social policy began on the frontier with the organization of the first band of vigilantes. It was negative social policy. Its aim was to stop abuse. Use, short of abuse, was ignored.

Most American social legislation has been written in the frontier tradition. Trust-busting had a vigilante flavor independent of the rough-rider costume of "T. R." The growth of trusts received no statutory notice.

The security of the pioneer in his clearing depended on his energy, his health, the weather, and the natural resources of the area where he lived. His standard of living could not be other than low. When his clearing and that of the next man to him expanded until their edges overlapped, the security of each became subject to the actions of the other. Their interdependence might create an enhanced standard of living for both of them. Or it might result in exploitation and subjugation of the one by the other.

The era of uncontrolled interdependence in American agriculture has at certain periods in our national history provided most American farmers with a standard of living superior to that obtainable on the frontier. At other periods, notably the recent period, its results have been:

Overstimulation of competition between more than six million individuals whose goods have left the self-sufficient clearing and entered a market economy which for some products is world-wide, with a resultant fall of farm prices below cost, and imbalance between farm prices and prices of other commodities;

Divorce between ownership and use in the case of nearly half the farms of the country.

The era of uncontrolled interdependence in American industry has at certain periods in our national history provided most American city dwellers with a standard of living superior to that obtainable on the frontier. At other periods, notably the recent period, its results have been:

Exposure of increasing portions of the nation's wealth and the nation's income to the ups and downs of the business cycle;

Concentration of effective control in the hands of a small minority, with a resultant dependence of the re-

What Is Security?

maining millions on the precarious proceeds of a competitive sale of their labor.

The era of interdependence in American economic life has of necessity forced the valuation of goods and services by a common monetary denominator. During certain periods the length of this measuring rod has remained substantially constant. During other periods, notably the recent period, its fluctuations have caused expropriation and appropriation of wealth, with corresponding shifts in the social situation of various classes and with notable effect on the savings of yesterday's workers to support today's old age.

Even in the independence of the clearing, the pioneer's security depended on the natural resources of the area in which he lived. In the interdependence of a settled continent, security is even more dependent on natural resources because they can be altered by group exploitation far more rapidly than by the individual alone.

The frontier tradition of not taking action until abuse reached sufficient proportions to rouse the vigilante spirit in the community has postponed to our own time consideration of our national resources with a view to constructive use. Today's dust in our eyes is the dust of the prairies where the frontier tradition was developed.

If the insecurity of interdependence continues as a chronic feature of American life, liberty will become for all, as it is now for many, impossible of realization.

Basic to the achievement of greater security for

the interdependent citizens of today's America is a changed attitude toward the use of our national resources, and toward the various categories of property under which their use is sanctioned by the State.

With regard to property-holding, there is no such thing as *an* American system. The American state sanctions the individual type of property-holding, say of homes or of farms, in which ownership, management, and operation are united in the same person. The American state sanctions the corporate type of property holding, say of manufacturing plants or distributive services, in which ownership, management and operation are divided among thousands and even hundreds of thousands of persons. The American state sanctions the government type of property-holding, say of schools or roads, in which ownership is by the public, and the necessary operations are performed by employees of the state.

The variety of work to be done in a society as complex as ours makes it highly desirable that different forms of property should exist. Farms are necessary to American security. So are factories. So is transportation. The means appropriate to the best use of national resources, however, are not necessarily the same for all types of resources. The question of what sorts of property-holding should be encouraged by the state should be discussed in relation to the best use of particular kinds of property.

And best use must be defined with a view to maintenance of access to property by the state for its citi-

What Is Security? 37

zens. Citizens without property can have no security. Citizens without security can have no liberty.

The speculative land-boom agriculture of the recent past has turned the majority of American farmers into a property-less class. The cost of this class is subject to economic reckoning in terms of soil erosion and loss of soil fertility in a nation that has already despoiled as many acres as are annually planted to crops within its borders.

The cost of the property-less class of farm tenants is subject to political reckoning in terms of potential support for a totalitarian state. Democracy has failed to maintain access to property for the body of citizenry of which such tenants form a part; their interest in political leaders who promise a share in the nation's wealth has already been demonstrated.

The effect of the current allocation and control of the proceeds of American industry is no less subject to economic and political reckoning than the effect of our current system of land use. Its economic effect is to keep industrial production markedly below the current capacity of an industrial plant which would have to be considerably enlarged to supply American citizens with the goods they require for a decent standard of living. Its political effect has been to force the appropriation, by both major parties, of national monies for relief. At the pit of the depression, revolution was recognized as the alternative to governmental acceptance of national responsibility for maintaining access to property—at least to the extent necessary for minimum subsistence—for all citizens.

But the provision of access to property for citizens on relief consisted in the handing out of government funds, of drafts, in other words, on the production of those for whom access to property still existed. To the extent to which this occurred the American state assumed the totalitarian function of supplying to part of its citizens the content of security rather than maintaining the conditions of access to property under which those citizens could seek their own security.

Citizens who look to the state for the major portion of the property on which their security depends cannot continue to exercise the freedom of opinion and action which a democracy requires. They lose their liberty, and jeopardize the democracy whose sanction of faulty property relationships has deprived them of security.

Maintenance of democracy for those American citizens now capable of participating in the democratic process, and restoration of the capacity to participate to the hundreds of thousands of citizens who lack the means today, requires revaluation of present-day property sanctions.

The current allocation of the nation's income and the control of the nation's wealth are outgrowths of certain property relationships. They are not, as some of our citizens are prone to assume, natural outgrowths of freedom under laissez faire. The property relationships upon which ownership, con-

WHAT IS SECURITY?

trol, and participation depend are state sanctioned and maintained by the collective forces of the community, acting according to directions given by the courts in applying the socially accepted body of law. (The person who thinks that the current arrangement of America's economic assets is the product of individual actions unaided by the sanctions of society would do well to ponder the use of the injunction in the history of American industry.)

A diffuse and reliable consuming power resulting from property possessed is indispensable to economic security in the United States. Which of the technics of property-holding now sanctioned lessen security? Which of the technics now sanctioned tend to bring our security closest to the limits which natural forces and resources impose upon it? Can we discover new technics for rendering available legitimate income from the nation's wealth?

The potential results of the diffusion of income through widening strata of the population can be indicated by the story of farm income and rural retail sales—sales, that is to say, of goods made by industrial workers whose employment put them also in a position to buy—from 1929 to 1935.

In 1929, farm cash income was $10,417,000,000; rural retail trade totaled $9,200,000,000. In 1932, income was $4,377,000,000 and trade was estimated at $3,900,000,000. In 1935, income was $6,900,000,000 and trade $6,700,000,000. Translation of these sales figures into production and employment figures indicates the extent to which increase in the consuming power of a low-income group brings the industrial productive capacity of the country into fuller use. And it must be remembered that these increases reflect only negligible changes in the incomes of the share tenants, croppers, and agricultural laborers who make up a large fraction of the rural population.

How can access to an improved standard of living be opened to these farmers?

Enactment of an American policy of land tenure is long overdue. The objective of the Homestead Acts, framed to establish family-sized farms owned by the people who farmed them, was lost in the speculative conversion of public property into private profits. The consequent destruction of public property is scrawled over the surface of the continent in the gullies of eroded land. The Bankhead-Jones Farm Tenant Bill is a restatement of the homestead objective.

Both from the standpoint of national resources and from the standpoint of the security of individual citizens of the American democracy, a system of individual ownership such as that which the Bankhead-Jones Bill would help to create, is preferable to the transient waste of tenancy as we now have it in many areas.

Ownership alone, however, is not enough. Ownership can free the farmer from the landlord's tolls upon his tenancy. It can secure to him the produce of his toil. But it cannot assure him that there will be much produce.

WHAT IS SECURITY? 41

Diffusion of income through the agricultural population requires not only a national policy of land tenure but a national policy of land use. Retirement of submarginal acres, coöperative farming of holdings too small to be economically efficient, and continual adjustment of production to market needs and land capacities are all prerequisites to the diffusion and maintenance of a reliable consuming power and hence economic security among our rural citizens.

Maintenance of access to an improved standard of living for city workers is likewise important to an improved standard of living on our farms. Unless the cities are able to buy, prices of farm products sag, and farm boys and girls, unable to find jobs in the cities, increase the pressure on livings earned from the land.

The importance of city jobs can be indexed by the fact that about two-thirds of the national income paid out every year takes the form of salaries, wages, and other labor payments. In 1935, about 36 of the 54 billion dollars of income paid out was paid to American citizens in return for their working time.

The requirements for maintaining security for urban workers differ materially from the requirements for maintaining security for workers on the land. Like most farm tenants, most city workers depend wholly on their labor for their livelihood. But while individual ownership, particularly if combined with certain coöperative practices, seems to be a desirable goal for farmers, individual ownership of the means of industrial production would throw us back to the inefficiencies of the period before applied science and render impossible the volume of production required for the diffusion of higher living standards.

The concentration of capital necessary to take advantage of modern technology has collectivized industrial production. The problem of tenure of the means of industrial production has by consequence assumed collective aspects.

The problem of industrial tenure has collective aspects in respect to the conditions under which modern corporate properties are held. It also has collective aspects in respect to the conditions under which are held the jobs that transmute the product of modern corporate properties into individual workers' incomes.

For the establishment of desirable conditions of tenure of the current corporate resources of the country, it is clearly necessary to develop a body of corporation law which fits the circumstances of modern business enterprise. Attention was called in the preceding chapter to the extent to which the *persona ficta* of the corporation had taken over the bundle of rights associated, in the preindustrial era, with the *persona realis* of the citizen. It has become increasingly clear during the past generation that the two legal categories of private property and public property are inadequate to cover the three realities of personal property, corporate property, and government property that characterize the current American scene.

What Is Security? 43

Considerable progress toward the establishment of a legal category of property intermediate between private and public has already been made. The law covering railroads as common carriers and the law covering the group of natural monopolies known as public utilities have defined economic areas in which public and private interests are both acknowledged. The depression has clarified the existence of other such areas by throwing light on the extent to which the production and price policies of one industry may affect other industries and the general economic situation. Law governing these areas should be developed industry by industry, as the law of common carriers and public utilities has been, in order that characteristic differences between industries may be fully taken into account. But the development of such law, correlating general with particular welfare, should proceed without delay.

Definition of desirable conditions of tenure of the nation's corporate resources must be paralleled by definition of desirable conditions of tenure of the nation's industrial jobs.

The collective operation of the parts of the economic system where modern technology has stimulated large capital outlay, whether such operation takes place under corporate, coöperative, or government tenure, involves a wage relationship on the part of hundreds of thousands of workers.

Maintenance of economic security among these wage-earners can be furthered: by recognizing the right to collective bargaining on the part of employees as a corollary to recognition of the fact of collective organization on the part of industry; and by providing a system of social insurances which offers citizens a means of maintaining their consuming power when regular sources of income fail, without jeopardy to their political independence.

Such action in the interest of economic security for industrial workers has to do with their lives as producers. The farmer both lives and works on his farm. The city dweller separates his life as a worker from his life as a consumer of the goods which his earnings supply. Outside factory hours, the city worker's problems of tenure take on forms familiar to workers on the land. The American dream of independent home owning is as unrealized in the city as in the country. Less than half of our entire citizen body consists of home owners. A policy of home ownership is as necessary a break with our speculative past in cities as on farms.

The foregoing policies are advanced as policies for farm and city which would facilitate achievement of the type of economic security which is compatible with the exercise of freedom, and which, in balance with freedom, would increase the liberty of the American citizenry.

It is clear that such policies must be closely coördinated with one another if they are to be effective. We want the type of society, we want the standard of living, which division of labor allows. But the security

What Is Security? 45

of interdependence, unlike the security of independence in a low-standard frontier society, or the security of dependence under absolutism, is the result of delicate interrelationships. Interrelationships between types of production, between groups, between regions, all affect the necessary balance. These interrelationships will not automatically remain in harmony. Successful social policy, in an interdependent society like ours, must concern itself with the total effect of current uses of national resources, and with the continuous, compensatory adjustments necessary to keep those uses in balance. So, and only so, can continuous access to property of a sort compatible with freedom be secured to the American people.

CHAPTER
FIVE

---- * ----

CAN THE UNION BE PRESERVED?

The Union of the United States of America is not an accident. It is an achievement. And it is an achievement for which a great price has been paid.

The Union cannot be taken for granted in the future any more than in the past. It cannot be taken for granted because some of the most powerful natural ties which other states rely upon to provide solidarity among their citizens are nonexistent in the United States. We are not one race. We do not have one religion. Only by a stretch of the imagination can we be called a nation. The size and diversity of our country is not favorable to concerted action.

What measure of unity we have had has been chiefly a by-product of two welding forces:

The welding force inherent in the task of occupying and developing a continent.

The welding force provided by what is often

described nowadays at the American dream or the American way of life.

The first of these forces is almost spent. The second represents great potential power if it could be revived and released. For the time being, however, its binding power is slight since the vision of life from which it springs has largely faded from the national consciousness.

The unity that remains is compounded of language, tradition, and trade. The unifying value of a common language is considerable if conflicting interests can be reconciled. Otherwise it is of no use whatever as the eighteen-sixties clearly demonstrated.

The tradition of Union in many sections of the United States is a positive force of immense significance. Where the Union was imposed by arms the tradition has been accepted, but it naturally lacks the flavor of spontaneity.

More substantial than language and more universal than tradition is the unity resulting from commercial activity. Countrywide systems of distribution based on mass production have converted half a continent into a single market. The unity of Americans is essentially a consumers' unity. Such unity seems stalwart enough during periods of prosperity. But its intrinsic fragility becomes apparent as soon as the nation is exposed to the strain of a long economic depression. When the consuming power of great sections of the population has been destroyed, national unity dependent upon a continent-wide consumers' market is destroyed with it. Market-place unity obviously does not constitute a bond of sufficient strength to ensure permanent union between the States. There is the further consideration that no nation ever achieved lasting greatness by relying on commercial activity to supply its common life with meaning.

If the above analysis is correct, the unity of the United States at the present time leaves much to be desired. It seems doubtful whether the national unity which we now possess is sufficient to provide us with a common sense of direction in place of our current chaos of desire or is adequate to stand the strain of the years ahead.

How can the Union be preserved? The Union can be preserved only if our commercial activities, our sectional interests, and our varying social traditions become increasingly subservient to a common moral purpose which transcends and conditions them. Only in this way will our national life acquire positive meaning and value sufficient to make men wish to preserve it for its own sake. The moral purpose to which Americans are most likely to give their allegiance can best be stated in terms of social justice.

The Union will continue as long as it serves as a symbol of social justice to the people who compose it. Since the amount of injustice which men will endure before rebelling is notorious, it would perhaps be truer to say that the Union will continue until it has become a positive symbol of injustice to a considerable number of citizens. The disintegration begins, however, long before the collapse occurs. The War between the States was incubating for more than half a century.

Disintegration of the Union commences whenever any section or class begins to suspect that benefits to be derived from membership in the Union are less than injuries incurred. If the economic security of millions of citizens is threatened or destroyed, those citizens naturally ask questions about the adequacy of the society of which they form a part. Their misfortune may have resulted from the operation of purely impersonal forces, or it may have resulted from greed masquerading under the name of liberty. In either case the victims of disaster tend to lose confidence in the existing social structure. And their loss of confidence is accelerated if it appears that misfortune came to them because of individual practices or public policies which enriched other sections or other classes at their expense. Nothing destroys national unity more effectively than the growing suspicion that one part of the country is exploiting another part or that wealth created by the labor of the citizens of one state provides luxury for the citizens of another state while the original producers remain in poverty.

If such a condition were to prevail over a long period of time the national unity of the United States conceived of in democratic terms would inevitably disappear. Fear and hatred would grow between section and section and between class and class. Increasing civil strife would result in the gradual break-up of national unity from within. At a certain point in the process of disintegration the only force strong enough to maintain a semblance of national unity would be armed force. And in the name of preserving the Union a dictator would arise to apply it.

If, on the other hand, the Union is preserved in a democratic sense and in a form which commands the loyalty of the mass of citizens, it will be because the people's sense of fair-play has been sufficiently aroused to ensure a rough approximation of social justice as between sections and as between producing groups. Our national character disposes us to imagine that social justice can be secured through emotional appeals and moral crusades. One would suppose that a century and a half of continuous disillusionment would be sufficient to cure us of attachment to this fallacy. Social justice of the kind we are discussing can only be realized through a genuine national policy to which the Federal and State governments are equally committed. This fact constitutes an urgent challenge to responsible citizens of both major parties.

The formulation of a national policy is essential to national well-being. The formulation of a national policy by means of a locally awakened democratic process is a condition of preserving the Union.

The urgency of developing a national policy is in direct proportion to the extent to which American society has acquired the character of a nation. For more than a hundred years after the adoption of our

Constitution the United States was not a nation. There was consequently no such thing as a national policy in the sense in which that term can now be employed. Such policies as appeared were generally policies favored by a geographic area, either by a state or by a section. Until 1860 the aim of the Federal Government was to maintain some kind of balance between divergent sectional policies. The War between the States put an end to the sectional balance of power. It put an end to it by destroying one of the sections. But it was a Pyrrhic victory. As happens in most wars, the real victor was not the apparent victor. The real victory was won not by the free institutions of the North and West but by the industrialist class. After 1865, government of the nation as a whole through the influence of one dominant class took the place of government based on a balance between sectional interests.

The triumph of the industrialist class insured the development of a strong and consistent national policy for more than two generations. It was a national policy not in the sense that it was in the interest of the nation but in the sense that it was imposed upon the nation. The strength of this policy was due in part to the singleness of its purpose. It had but one objective, the aggrandizement of industry. But the ruling industrialists were too unimaginative to see the eventual consequences of their aggrandizement.

Under the protectionist policy of the industrialist class the agrarian South and Middle West have been annually impoverished by having to sell their agricultural products in the low-priced world market while buying their manufactured goods in the high-priced protected domestic market. The industrialists have exploited both the South and the Middle West as if these sections of the country were part of a colonial empire.

The exploitation of the South has been so thorough that hundreds of thousands of whites as well as blacks now occupy a position economically inferior to the position occupied by many slaves prior to 1861. In view of the outcome of the War between the States exploitation of the South was no doubt to be expected.

Exploitation of the Middle West was, however, hardly to be expected. That section furnished some of the best troops for the Union armies. Yet it was immediately betrayed by its war-time industrial allies of the East. That the Middle Western farmers, after being betrayed, should have remained for the most part politically loyal to their betrayers for two-thirds of a century is an extraordinary instance of an alliance whose sentimental strength was such that it persisted long after the alliance itself ceased to have any relation to realities and in spite of the fact that the interests of one of the principal allies were actually repudiated by the terms of the alliance.

During the nineteen-twenties, however, this situation was altered by the development of an agrarian pressure group bent on securing, through such devices as the McNary-Haugen Bill or the export debenture plan, an equivalent to the protection which the industrial pressure group had successfully maintained through the tariff. The strength of this movement in the nineteen-thirties has been evidenced in the economic sphere by the passage of the Agricultural Adjustment Act and in the political sphere by the shift of the center of operations of the Republican Party to the Mississippi basin.

The cleavage between the agricultural and the industrial forces is a cleavage between both economic groups and geographic sections.

A second cleavage, which has been developing in importance even more recently than that between industry and agriculture, is the cleavage between industry and labor. For nearly two generations, Samuel Gompers' decision to oppose the formation of a labor party and to support the formation of craft unions has localized the pressures applied by American labor. The rise of industrial unionism, its growth through the nineteen-twenties, the encouragement given to organization by various Acts of the New Deal, and the formation of the Committee for Industrial Organization in 1935 have materially increased American working class solidarity.

The cleavage between the labor and the big business forces, except in the case of industries moved to agricultural areas but managed from business centers, is a cleavage between economic groups rather than geographic sections, but its importance to the maintenance of union is no less on that account.

The rise of agrarianism and of industrial unionism alike signal the beginning of the end of the control of government by the industrialist class.

But it would be a great mistake to suppose that the industrialist class will return to the nation without a struggle the sovereignty which it has taken from the nation. After fairly continuous rule for seventy years the industrialist class has developed the cohesion and self-consciousness of an aristocracy. The probable emergence of such an aristocracy was foreseen by John Taylor of Caroline County, Virginia, more than a century ago. In his *An Inquiry into the Principles and Policy of the Government of the United States*, he wrote:

> Thus law charters, with the faithless design of enslaving a nation by the introduction of the aristocracy of the present age, crouch behind the good and honest words "publick faith and national credit," to prevent a nation from destroying that, which is destroying it.... By admitting that donations of public property by a government to individuals, should irrevocably transform it into private property, it is obvious that the stock of publick rights will be continually whittled away. Tyranny is only a partial disposition of publick rights, in favour of one or a few. The system of paper and patronage, bottomed upon charters and commissions, enables avarice and ambition to draw more extensively upon the national stock than any system hitherto invented. It can convert publick property into private, with unexampled rapidity, or transfer wealth and power from the mass of a nation to a few ... every species of fraud, monopoly and usurpation call the pillages of private property, private property, and generally contrive to make it so by laws or armies.

CAN THE UNION BE PRESERVED? 55

The pseudo-aristocracy of "paper and patronage" which John Taylor foresaw might one day menace free institutions in America is no longer a subject for prophecy. It exists and in fact has existed long enough to acquire some of the subtlety of age. It has learned that the exercise of its control over the government depends upon the maintenance of a façade of free institutions behind which it can assert its minority rule by indirection.

The maintenance of genuinely free institutions, as contrasted with this façade, depends upon policy consciously formulated and administered to create and preserve a balance between interests, in the place of policy which connives in the dominance of special interests. The creation and preservation of this balance is the essence of sound national policy.

The first period of American history was characterized by sectional policy and the second period by class policy. It remains to be seen whether the third period will be characterized by national policy. Some currents of American life seem to be flowing in the direction of national policy; others seem to be flowing away from it. It is too soon to predict which will prove the stronger.

The New Deal at its best is an expression of forces making for a national policy based on social justice. That is the reason why the Republicans have been compelled to compete with the Democrats in adopting New Deal language and objectives.

On the other hand, there are powerful latent forces

which may make the realization of an effective national policy increasingly difficult. Among these is the new spirit of sectionalism which is appearing in different parts of the country. Many different factors have contributed to the creation of this new sectionalism. There is, for example, the growing appreciation of the distinctive assets of the different regions and a realization of the fact that until each region makes the fullest and wisest use of its own resources it cannot make its largest contribution to the life of the nation. This positive and constructive regionalism has found expression in the monumental study of Howard Odum, *Southern Regions*.

There are indications, however, of a mood in different parts of the country which is less constructive than this positive type of regionalism. Negative sectionalism has its roots in fear that the Union as a whole may not be interested in assuring social and economic justice to its several parts. It also represents the natural logic of the argument for economic nationalism. Autarchy is an ironic deity who delights in destroying her devotees by blinding them with excessive faith. After passing through Mr. Beard's Open Door at Home (Home meaning the country as a whole), the advocates of economic nationalism find themselves successively passing through the Open Door of the Section, the Open Door of the State, and the Open Door of the Locality. As they pass through, the doors close behind. "The South must live off its own industries." "State public buildings must be built out of

State materials." "You may be an American citizen but if you haven't legal settlement in this county you don't get relief." Economic nationalism works only too well. It ends by evoking a spirit which destroys the economy of the nation.

Because the new sectionalism has few precedents to go by, it manifests itself in a wide variety of shapes and forms. It may express itself in the vague but profound suspicion which so many Middle Westerners feel toward anything which originates in the East. The Republican party has been sufficiently impressed by this sentiment to carry the search for a candidate west of the river. In the Pacific Northwest the Washington Commonwealth Federation owes part of its appeal to the spirit of sectionalism. In the South this spirit clamors for expression through such groups as the Nashville Agrarians or the Southern Policy Association.

For the time being the significance of such phenomena is merely symptomatic. There is no immediate danger of a Balkanized North America. But there is danger in the long run unless national policy guarantees justice as between regions and groups and so produces a positive desire to preserve the Union.

CHAPTER
SIX

———————— ✶ ————————

CAN DEMOCRACY FUNCTION ON A CONTINENTAL SCALE?

THE UNION AND THE BLESSINGS OF LIBERTY ARE NOT realities which have an existence of their own independent of the structure and procedure of government. On the contrary the structure and procedure of government are directly related to the preservation of the Union and the enjoyment of liberty. Every important act of an administration has the effect of either weakening or strengthening the Union, of making the blessings of liberty either more available or less available. And sometimes inaction is even more decisive than action. What is true of action on the part of the administration is equally true of legislation on the part of Congress and of constitutional interpretation on the part of the Supreme Court.

The structure and procedure of government will naturally vary from country to country according to the political theory on which government is based and according to the size and geographic features of the country to be governed. For us in the United States the structure and procedure of government are conditioned by our desire to make representative political institutions function throughout a continental territory whose geographic subdivisions are large enough and varied enough to constitute nations in their own right. In other words the size and variety of the territory of the United States compel us to reëxamine the conditions which have to be fulfilled if democratic government is to operate successfully. Heretofore, democracies, if they have succeeded at all, have succeeded in relatively small areas. The larger the area the more likely a dictator. Is it possible that we can succeed where others have failed? Can we make democracy work across a continent?

The bearing of the size of the United States upon the problem of American government is well illustrated by an examination of non-governmental social forces whose power depends upon the extent of American territory over which it is possible for them to operate. Since the political structure of the United States was built on a continental scale it was inevitable that the structure of American industry and trade should also be built on the same scale. But as soon as specific industries acquired continental proportions it was obviously no longer possible for the several states to express the "public interest" in relation to those industries. The corporate organization of the latter, extending from coast to coast, was capable of mobilizing social power greater than any single state or any group of neighboring states could possibly mobilize.

Indeed the power of some of these self-contained economic empires has occasionally been so great that they were capable of defying and for brief periods even of controlling policies of the Federal Government. Yet the Federal Government is the only agency which can say what the interest of the nation as a whole is in relation to any particular continent-wide structure of industry or trade.

This situation makes it obvious that if democracy is to function successfully on a continental scale, the structure, procedure, and powers of the Federal Government must be fashioned to achieve this end. Definite criteria can be applied to determine whether or not the Federal Government is equipped for such a task. What are some of these criteria?

Does the Federal Government encourage the democratic process of policy-making and is it sensitive to the recommendations evolved out of that process?

The nature of the democratic process was described in May, 1935, by Richard F. Cleveland in language that deserves careful study. Mr. Cleveland wrote:

> The democratic process contemplated and made effective by the founders of American institutions not only provides the *right* of every citizen to participate in the process, but presumes the *duty* of *active* participation if the continuation of that process is to be assured. Democracy thrives insofar as its roots are deep, that is, insofar as the votes of elected representatives reflect continuing participation of citizens in the process at its source. When

Democracy: Continental Scale

the process of participation breaks down the substance of democratic institutions disappears, though the form may remain. This process is valid and desirable in itself; it is worth preserving even though some form of dictatorship may be more efficient mechanically. It is far more important to cultivate the individual than to promote mere machine-like efficiency through a dictatorship, which by definition implies the relative devaluation of human beings.

There are people everywhere in the United States, today, who are eager to participate in forming policies, but who have no available organ of articulation. While many citizens are indifferent or preoccupied, a very substantial number are isolated and wasted merely because there is no conduit through which their efforts can flow into the democratic policy-forming process. The reasons for this isolation at present are clear.

In the first place, the Federal Executive, surrounded by experts, formulates measures and makes them effective by his dominance over Congress. Part of this dominance, at least, derives from the power of patronage, and nearly all of it comes under the head of party discipline. Quite apart from whether such measures are abstractly sound, they obviously do not develop out of a democratic process. The fact is that many such measures are wholly unintelligible, if only because the people have no opportunity to cogitate them before they are soothingly handed out as *faits accomplis*. This statement does not necessarily condemn the President for taking drastic action in an emergency; it only points out that there is a widening gap between the Executive and the people, which has resulted in the creation of a vacuum into which every kind of charlatan and demagogue may rush. The following of Father Coughlin, for instance, whatever its other aspects, demonstrated how ready the unstable and disillusioned were to rush into such a vacuum behind plausible leadership. In other countries we have seen movements such as this attain national dimensions and furnish material for national dictatorships, whose necessary first step toward self-preservation is the abolition of the democratic process.

Furthermore, while the country is today honeycombed with citizens' movements of every kind, some of which are sincere, nearly all of them are frankly concerned with a special narrow interest as contrasted with national interest. At the same time, the two major political parties do not provide in their attitudes or in their machinery material from which the democratic process can be fashioned. The Democrats today have almost no coherent principles; their party has largely become a vast machine for administering patronage and maintaining discipline, with practically no other common purpose, tradition or belief. The Republican Party has so far been able to find no appealing issue around which even conservatives may rally, and notoriously includes individuals whose divergence of views could not be more marked.

This national situation obviously constitutes a breakdown of democratic institutions, at a time when interest in public questions is more lively than for many years.

The democratic process described by Mr. Cleveland presupposes:

The availability of accurate and concise information regarding issues of national importance.

The existence of local, state, and regional groups composed of responsible citizens who will use this information to clarify their own opinions and to formulate recommendations on policy.

The existence of legislative and executive branches of the government responsive to this nation-wide process of discussion and formulation.

The democratic process is essentially a two-way process. The movement one way consists of the voluntary opinions and activities of citizens converging on Washington. The movement the other way consists of the response of government to these activities and its outreach to stimulate citizens to further thought and action. Considering the distance between the Atlantic and the Pacific and between the Canadian Border and the Gulf it is apparent that special attention needs to be given both by citizens acting in their private capacity and by government acting in its official capacity to the creation of channels for this two-way process between Washington and the local electorates.

The attitude of the party in power at any one time toward the democratic process determines to a considerable extent what chance that process has of functioning effectively. If an administration ignores this process out of preference for policy made by experts on its staff, the masses of the people, through sheer neglect, are bound to become increasingly occupied with freakish issues. As a result, members of Congress get confused by the concern of their constituents for irrelevancies, and so a "must" program becomes necessary to clear the legislative calendars. But "must" programs are the utter denial of the democratic process.

It cannot be said with too much emphasis, however, that it is not the function of a federal administration to attempt to establish a monopoly over the supply of factual information required by the democratic process or to supervise the citizens' use of such information in formulating policy. But it is the function of an administration to make it clear to the country that it relies upon that process for its own sense of direction. The natural predilections of the American people are such that the democratic process will still work if a president wants it to work. The responsibility of the president is, therefore, correspondingly great.

Does the Federal Government provide responsible and efficient administration?

Sound administration is essential to good government in the smallest country. It is indispensable in a country the size of the United States. The larger the country the greater the likelihood of waste through confusion, duplication, and useless experimentation.

If confidence in democratic institutions is to continue, there must be responsible administration of government. This means that administrators must be held responsible for the specific tasks assigned them. It is the duty of Congress to exercise its control over the public funds in such a way that this responsibility will be assured. Responsibility implies accountability as to funds, continuity as to records, and consistency as to policy.

The president is responsible for himself. He is also responsible for his administrators. Excessive grants of unspecified spending power to the president are a menace to democratic institutions. No man is good enough and no crisis is great enough to justify such grants. They encourage irresponsible government. They encourage government by the whim and fancy of men rather than by clearly understood and publicly declared rules of administration. The moment Congress makes grants for which strict accountability cannot be required it surrenders a prerogative which has been rightly regarded as the essential safeguard of free institutions.

Has the Federal Government adequate sovereignty?

In a country whose vast extent permits small groups of private citizens to acquire tremendous economic and financial power, it is necessary for government to possess correspondingly greater power. Otherwise sovereignty passes from the state to private corporations and the masses of the people lack an organ which has sufficient authority to declare the public interest on their behalf.

The Federal Government requires sufficient sovereignty to assure to citizens their right to exercise freedom and their right of access to the means of acquiring security.

The Federal Government requires sufficient sovereignty to preserve the balance between freedom and security. It requires sufficient sovereignty to preserve this balance in every section of the country and among all sections of the population.

The Federal Government requires sufficient sovereignty to preserve a balance in standards of living between sections of the country and between sections of the population (as for example between farmers and industrialists).

Our Federal Government is commonly described as

a government of delegated powers. It has become increasingly obvious that the Supreme Court's recent attempts to define the powers delegated to the Federal Government leave that Government with insufficient sovereignty to make democratic institutions work on a continental scale. The several states are unable to exercise the theoretical sovereignty they possess and the Federal Government is told that it cannot exercise sovereignty because it does not possess it. If the definition of the Supreme Court is accepted there is no government in the United States in which at the present time sufficient sovereignty resides to enable it to fulfill its obligations to the people.

Another way of saying this is that great segments of the nation's economic life have been fenced off into private preserves. The courts themselves have nailed up "Posted" signs, not for the purpose of warning off trespassing marauders but for the purpose of keeping out officers of the law. The Government of the United States has no right of access to these preserves. Within them the law of the jungle is the law of the land. Women factory workers can be sweated, children can be deformed by overwork, and men be terrorized and assaulted by company thugs. All of this is done in the name of freedom. The conscience of the nation is outraged, but the nation can do nothing about it.

This is a very dangerous situation. If in a time of rapid social change the powers of government are weaker than the powers exercised by organized groups of private citizens, the possibility of social disintegration and disaster is greatly increased. The greatest danger of all lies in the fact that as long as this situation continues, the executive, faced by the necessity of acting when he possesses no clear constitutional mandate for action, is driven to resort to subterfuge and evasion to accomplish what the Government ought to be able to accomplish by the exercise of powers clearly delegated to it. Under the Constitution of 1787 the Federal Government possesses sufficient power to accomplish the purposes enumerated above. But for the present the Government is prevented by the Supreme Court from exercising these powers. Consequently it becomes the duty of the people to take whatever steps may be necessary to restore to the Federal Government its freedom to exercise its sovereignty. And it becomes the duty of the President to prepare public opinion for taking these steps.

Has the Federal Government sufficient restraint not to arrogate to itself functions which could be better performed by smaller units of government?

The Federal Government requires freedom to exercise the powers delegated to it because of the continent-wide structure of industry and finance. It needs this power in order to express the public interest through an effective national policy. But the exercise of further power, however necessary it may be, creates new dangers as well as confers new benefits.

There is danger of excessive centralization resulting in the vices of bureaucracy, and there is corresponding danger of diminution of the sense of local responsibility. In order to avoid these dangers the exercise of additional power should be accompanied by devolution of certain types of Federal administration onto state and regional units.

The question of whether the Federal Government has sufficient restraint to devolve administrative functions in this way is not a question which the administrators themselves can be trusted to answer. An able and aggressive executive naturally prefers to have the levers of control close at hand. Provision for such devolution will depend upon Congressional action.

There are of course other criteria which ought to be applied to the Federal Government to determine whether it is equipped to make democracy work on a continental scale. Are the actual interests, for example, of the varied regions and groups which compose the nation adequately represented in Congress? Does the present method of congressional representation constitute the most satisfactory method of securing an expression of public opinion regarding national policy? Many questions of a similar nature might be asked. But a sufficient number of criteria have probably been mentioned to make the point clear that the structure and procedure of the Federal Government cannot be taken for granted. If democratic institutions are to survive and function, the structure and procedure of government must be adjusted to the requirements of those institutions as they attempt to express themselves in continental terms. This is a condition of securing the blessings of liberty.

CHAPTER
SEVEN

———————— * ————————

LIBERTY UNDER THE NEW DEAL

How has Liberty fared under the New Deal? Has the New Deal increased the number of citizens who can exercise their freedom because they have access to the means of acquiring security? Has the New Deal helped to maintain a better balance between security and freedom? Has the New Deal helped to make democratic institutions function more satisfactorily on a continental scale? The scope of this paper does not permit a thorough critique of the New Deal. These questions will be discussed briefly merely for the sake of illustrating the problem of government with which responsible American citizens are concerned at the present time.

The New Deal is compounded of an Administration and a Party. The Administration includes the Executive and a majority in both houses of Congress. It is assumed that the constitutional function of Con-

LIBERTY UNDER THE NEW DEAL 71

gress is to declare national policy and the constitutional function of the Executive is to advise Congress regarding policy and then put into effect the policy which Congress declares. The policy declared by Congress is presumed to reflect the principles of the Party in power. More important than either the Administration or the Party are the People in whom, as recognized by the Constitution, final sovereignty resides. The record of liberty under the New Deal is the record of the contribution of these three elements in government to the American balance between security and freedom.

THE ADMINISTRATION

The rôle of the New Deal executive in securing the blessings of liberty constitutes one of the most striking paradoxes in American history. No Administration has aroused greater hopes among the mass of the people or released more liberal economic and social trends. And the same Administration which has aroused these liberal hopes and released these liberal trends has relied for its power upon some of the country's most illiberal political machines. By its patronage it has reënforced reaction in order to secure reform.

The positive achievements of the Administration are sufficient to bear comparison with the achievements of any preceding Administration. Through the AAA program the balance has been partially restored between farm income (as far as land owners and cash tenants are concerned) and industrial income. The TVA has already functioned long enough to demonstrate that the type of organization which it represents is capable of supplying electric power more cheaply than the traditional type of utility. Consequently it is making available for rural communities a standard of living which every section of the country will learn to expect and know how to secure.

Industrial workers have been taught to anticipate a larger share in the national income and have been encouraged to organize in order to ensure an adequate wage scale with fair conditions of labor. Industrialists and financiers who think in terms of national welfare have been given the opportunity to collaborate with each other and with labor for the purpose of coördinating their own economic and financial policies with the total national policy. At the same time the licentious freedom of financiers and industrialists who in the name of liberty have placed their own good before the nation's good has been considerably curtailed. This is solid achievement. And it is achievement of a very high order. It means that far more citizens are able to exercise their freedom in 1936 than were able to exercise it in 1932 because far more citizens now have some access to the means of acquiring economic security. In this respect the New Deal has served the interests of liberty well.

But there is another side to the picture. This other side completes the paradox. It appears in all sections

LIBERTY UNDER THE NEW DEAL 73

of the country, and it can be illustrated by trends in the South.

The South has probably benefited from the New Deal more than any other section. Federal relief has been dispensed there with a lavish hand; in proportion to the amounts supplied locally no other region has received so much from the national treasury. After seventy-five years of tariff exploitation and the consequent poverty of the section there is a measure of justice in this. But though the South's gains under the New Deal have been great, the losses have also been great. For the New Deal has materially strengthened groups which would like nothing better than to see the liberal democratic movement in the South sold down the river.

The income of the landowner has improved under the AAA. But the position of the share-tenant and the share-cropper (who constitute more than half of the farmers of the Cotton Belt) has not. Some authorities say that the operation of the AAA has made the condition of these more than a million farmers definitely worse. Many never received the benefit payments to which they were entitled. Others were evicted because of acreage reduction despite provisions to the contrary in the Act. The record of southern relief rolls gives evidence of the prevalence of this practice.

In the light of these facts it is not surprising that there should be signs of growing unrest among the agricultural masses in different parts of the Deep

South. The causes of this unrest are as complex as southern history. Among immediate causes which deserve attention is the policy of the former Cotton Section of the AAA. The Cotton Section of the AAA preferred to forget that there were tenants and sharecroppers. It administered its control program as if it were a landlord's "code," and thereby set the stage for increasing agricultural conflict. Periodic outbreaks of violence in Arkansas are a tribute to the Cotton Section's lack of political foresight and intelligence. And the administration of the old Cotton Section is the same as the administration of the new Southern Region of the AAA under the Soil Conservation Act.

Under the New Deal the agricultural masses in the South have been largely ignored except for some excellent but scattered experiments undertaken by the Resettlement Administration. The only recognition which these forgotten men have had came in the form of a verbal sop in the Philadelphia platform which recognized "the gravity of the evils of farm tenancy." The value of this belated recognition may be estimated by recalling the history of the Bankhead-Jones Farm Tenant Bill. That Bill was a move in the direction of genuine land reform. It passed the Senate in 1935. But it never came out of the House Committee on Agriculture. Why? Because the New Deal lacked the political power to get the Bill out.

This is an indication of the price the President has paid for maintaining regular machine relations with some of his most intransigent opponents. He has connived in the recognition of these gentlemen as members in good standing of the Democratic Party. He has fortified their intransigence by his patronage. And in the end he has lost whatever semblance of control he may have once established over the Democratic Party in the South. It was too great a price to pay. Besides it was unnecessary. The Administration could have broken with the more reactionary state machines and still carried every southern state in November.

The situation in the South is not unique. It reveals a structural weakness in the New Deal that may yet prove disastrous. The superstructure of the New Deal is in many of its features admirable. There are faults, but the faults are insignificant in comparison with the merits of the general design. The superstructure, however, rests on foundations which are thoroughly insecure. In fact large sections of these foundations are so rotten that they are already crumbling. Foundations in this condition are manifestly incapable of supporting an enduring national policy. This is the essence of the New Deal paradox.

If Mr. Roosevelt is reëlected it remains to be seen whether he can repair the foundations sufficiently to ensure that the work of his Administration will endure. If he fails to effect the repairs the work of his Administration will not endure regardless of his reelection.

The dangers inherent in this New Deal paradox have been further accentuated by weaknesses in the executive itself.

The President could have prepared the people for a rational and enlightened consideration of the constitutional issues which the circumstances of national life have raised. He has not done this. Instead he has trusted to his own unsurpassed political intuition to discover what was practicable, and has preferred to reserve the legislative formulation of the practicable to his own immediate advisers. In doing this the President has been doubly at fault. He has weakened the democratic process through disuse and has arrogated the policy-making function of the legislative arm of government to the executive arm of government.

Nor has the administrative procedure of the executive increased the likelihood of democracy's being able to function successfully on a continental scale. The President is a brilliant but not a sound administrator. This can be explained in part by the degree to which his judgment is often warped by his relish for putting over a fast one.

Most of the New Deal agencies were attached to regular departments of the government and the quality of their administration depended upon the department in question. This is not true of relief. There the President has been in direct control. And there the largest funds are expended. The administrative record of relief constitutes, therefore, the most accurate gauge of the President's administrative ability. The story of relief is a continuous record of unstable administration. Both consistent policy and long-range planning have been conspicuously absent. Indeed changes in policy have occurred from day to day in such rapid succession that it has often been impossible for responsible executive officers to agree among themselves as to what the policy was which they were supposed to carry out. The result has been continuous confusion and immense waste. Mr. Hopkins has very loyally accepted full responsibility for this chaos. But Mr. Hopkins is not primarily responsible for it. That responsibility rests squarely upon the President.

Good administration involves persons as well as procedures. The appointments and activities of Mr. Moley and Mr. Peek illustrate the President's capacity to disregard the rudimentary conditions which have to be fulfilled if administrative machinery is to function efficiently.

Enough has been said to indicate the difficulty of estimating whether the New Deal as it stands today has increased or decreased the blessings of liberty. The short-range effect of its program seems in general to be on the positive side. How far are these short-range benefits jeopardized by long-range effects which have not yet been disclosed? The future alone can supply the answer.

If the New Deal ends in November this at least can be said: the New Deal has helped to create social forces which will some day discover an instrument through which they can build a more secure foundation for social justice in the United States. These forces, in fulfilling their mission, will destroy many of the instruments employed by the New Deal. That is perhaps a part of the irony of history.

If Mr. Roosevelt is reëlected it would be wiser to postpone any attempt to make a final estimate until 1940. The President likes to compare his strategy with the strategy of a quarterback. That is a good analogy provided there are rules to the game and the quarterback knows where the goal is. Occasionally it has been difficult to avoid the suspicion that the New Deal Quarterback was not too familiar with the rules and enjoyed playing the game as if his goal were at both ends of the field at the same time. One would prefer to believe that the President in his second term, freed from the necessity of paying close attention to immediate political considerations, would display more familiarity with the rules and would be surer of the exact location of his goal.

In any event the convinced liberal has no choice but to hope that Mr. Roosevelt will have the chance to demonstrate between 1937 and 1940 that he has learned the rules, that he knows his goal and that he can play the game.

Any discussion of liberty under New Deal government would obviously be incomplete without at least a brief reference to the Supreme Court and the Constitution. During the past year or two the majority of the Supreme Court has assumed the rôle of Cato the Censor. This majority has functioned almost exclusively as a sovereign veto agency over the other two presumably coequal branches of government. Because

LIBERTY UNDER THE NEW DEAL 79

of the powers delegated to it the Supreme Court has the responsibility of clarifying the intent of the Constitution with regard to freedom and the general welfare. As a result of its veto-mindedness it has been unable to fulfil that responsibility.

This negative inhibition which has blighted the Court's creative powers may be partially explained by the fact that the economic and legal world in which the majority of the Court lives is the world of the late nineteenth century. The decisions of this majority are attempts to explain how an eighteenth-century Constitution applies to twentieth-century actualities in terms of nineteenth-century economic theories, though these theories are as unrelated to the Constitution as they are to the problems of 1936. Consequently the assumptions on which the majority of the Court operates are inapplicable to the facts with which they have to deal. Instead of clarifying the intent of the Constitution with regard to freedom and the general welfare, recent decisions have further obscured it, with the result that the nation as a whole is becoming increasingly confused regarding the purpose which the Constitution is supposed to serve.

The use of the Court's veto power is obviously desirable where legislation has been hastily drawn or where it confers powers on the Federal Government which cannot be deduced from the language and intent of the Constitution. It is the Court's proper function to say that this or that particular method adopted by the Congress is not the method allowed by the Constitution for safeguarding the rights of citizens to exercise their freedom by enabling them to have access to the means of acquiring economic security. But the majority members of the present Court have gone much further than that. They have declared in effect that neither the Federal Government nor the governments of the several states have the power to ensure freedom for the mass of the people by facilitating their access to the means of acquiring economic security. They have even gone out of their way to give the impression that they did not believe this should be the function of government and that in any event they were unalterably opposed to its becoming the function of the American Government.

Insofar as the majority of the Court has embodied such sentiments in its decisions, the Court has ceased to be a judicial tribunal. To that extent the judicial arm of government, like the executive arm, has arrogated to itself functions delegated by the Constitution to the legislative arm. It is the responsibility of the Congress to take back what has been taken from it.

The fundamental guarantee of the Constitution is that the blessings of liberty shall be accessible to the mass of the people. Decisions of the Court which deprived government of the power to protect this guarantee would in effect destroy the Constitution. If the Court wishes to save the Constitution the only way it can do so is to render decisions which throw some light on what is the constitutional method of securing the blessings of liberty. The minority of the Court is performing this function.

If the 1935-1936 decisions of the Court were the last word, the nation would be put into a straitjacket from which it could no more escape without civil violence than it could escape after the Dred Scott decision of 1857. If the unwritten Constitution developed toward the end of the nineteenth century is what these decisions say it is, the only alternatives to eventual violence are changes in the Court's personnel through natural causes, or constitutional amendments which will bring our unwritten Constitution in line with the original written Constitution.

The Party

The public organs of government, the Congress, the President and the Supreme Court, have as their functions the declaration, the execution and the maintenance of national policy. Fulfilment of these functions presupposes the formulation of policy.

In a democratic country where liberty exists, formulation of policy is a quasi-private, quasi-public process, related on the one hand to the personal freedom of the individual citizen to think, speak and print, and on the other to the purposes of government formally declared in the Constitution and rendered effective by the public agencies for whose establishment it provides. This quasi-private, quasi-public process is institutionalized in the political party.

The recent history of American political parties bears little relation to the above definition. We have not had a national policy, and the bodies which might have made it have been busy with other matters. Patronage, not policy, has been the center of party interest.

Prior to 1932 the dominant American parties were not national parties. They were confederations of local interests. The relatively unimportant statements which they advanced as contributions to national policy were totals rather than wholes, being, in fact, points of equilibrium in the swapping and log-rolling activities of the heads of local machines. National policy was a policy of drift, disturbed occasionally by uncoördinated movements in inconsistent directions.

The Democratic Party that assembled at the Chicago Convention of 1932 was a party made on this model. The Democratic Party that assembled at the Philadelphia Convention of 1936 showed obvious changes. The activities of the national executive during the intervening years had gone far towards nationalizing the party.

The national character of the depression crisis rendered the need for a national policy imperative. In the imperative, a national policy was supplied.

The coinage—and immediate currency—of the word "brains trust" signaled the application of new faculties to the nation's problems. With the assembling of the President's advisers, a new policy-formulating body was created. This body assumed the function which the political parties of the country had long failed to exercise.

Inauguration of the brains trust's policies was followed by national activity in fields where party machines were at home. The dizzy millions applied to nationally organized public works and nationally organized relief offered a counter-attraction to the precinct type of social service on which local bosses were accustomed to base their followings. The focus of interest was on Washington. Federal connections became necessary to maintain local prestige. Under Farley the confederation of local interests became one big union.

The machine that was exhibited at Philadelphia showed how far the streamlining of the old bandwagon had gone in the last four years.

For the first time, state and city bosses milled in the mass unnoticed and unsought. Among the gazoo-tooting thousands, unprecedented numbers were federal officeholders. The crowd's interest in the antics of the sound machine surpassed its interest as to which truth it was holding self-evident while it cheered. One final cheer, superbly stage-managed at Franklin Field, and the Convention was over.

Neither behind the scenes nor on the floor was there discussion of the state of the nation. Of policy-making at Philadelphia there was none. The Convention was a sounding board, reflecting with enhanced volume ideas penned by the executive arm.

The spectacle was disquieting. How much difference, except in the matter of orderliness, would a man from Mars have seen between the Democratic Convention and demonstrations of Party response in the European dictatorships? Important differences do exist; but there are also important similarities.

Under the Roosevelt administration, the government has for the first time in several generations had the advice of numbers of men capable of viewing public affairs on a national scale. The advantage, indeed the necessity, of such an approach to the formulation of policy is obvious. But so long as the group of advisers is solely an appendage of the executive, the result of their deliberations is policy for the nation, not national policy.

The President's advisers are rootless individuals. They have no local habitation; no constituency in the country. As a result, when Congress practices trust-busting on the brains trust, the country is inclined to cheer; the tassel of a mortar-board does not look like a human scalp.

Maintenance of the democratic form of government in this country depends upon revival of policy-making through use of the democratic process. The channel of representation from the people of the United States to the Congress of the United States, from the free thought, speech, and print of the individual citizen to the policy-declaring body of the Federal Government must be the channel through which the main streams of national policy flow if democratic form is to be filled with democratic content. Pipelines from the White House to the Hill may have had their value as emergency public works, in view of previous clogging of the normal channel. But pipe lines notoriously lend themselves to monopoly.

The Roosevelt administration, in the 1932 crisis, collected a group of people who were capable of, and interested in, the formation of national policy. But the Roosevelt administration's concern with the Democratic Party has been to weld local party machines into a national machine to amplify the voice of the executive.

The administration has not made an effort to relate its advisory group to the party. It has not even made an effort to relate its advisory group to the current revival of citizen interest in public affairs. As a condition of liberty, establishment of those relations is a pressing task.

THE PEOPLE

It has been the repeated assertion of this pamphlet that the function of government in a democracy is to maintain the balance between freedom and security prerequisite to the enjoyment of liberty by the citizens.

Behind that assumption lies a prior assumption. Enjoyment of liberty by the citizens of a democracy is contingent upon exercise of their liberties. Freedom of thought, speech, press, and assembly are meaningless rights unless the citizens exercising them can put content into what is thought, spoken, printed, and conveyed, and can bear a responsible relationship to its consequences. Access to property is unimportant in the absence of an energetic desire on the part of the citizen to take advantage of economic opportunity and bear a responsible relationship to that part of the nation's wealth which, for a span of years, is his possession.

This prior assumption was a harsh reality to Americans of the founding period. Succeeding generations sentimentalized it; the growing economic oligarchy ignored it. Current events have made it a harsh reality again.

The functioning of the best of constitutions depends upon the quality of life of the people for whom it supplies the framework of government. An earlier chapter emphasized the fact that the search for economic security is only one part of the search for security. Capacity to use the material resources basic to economic security is conditioned by judgments, by values, and by those qualities which we associate with character, whose determination and achievement lie outside the field of economics and outside the field of government. Capacity to use the rights known as civil liberties is similarly conditioned.

The practice of democracy assumes a quality of life equal to the demands made upon citizens under a democratic constitution. It assumes affirmative answers to the twin questions: is a sufficient body of citizens capable of a thoughtful and responsible relationship to national policy, and is a sufficient body of citizens capable of an active and responsible relationship to the nation's wealth?

Is such an assumption valid today in these United States? What is the record of the people of the United States in face of the economic and political exigencies of the depression and the New Deal?

The followings of the late Huey Long, of Father Coughlin, and Dr. Townsend illustrate the irresponsibility of the dispossessed. Depression losses of life savings, and a prospect of unwelcome dependency for the rest of their days, have led millions of aging and aged all over the country to offer political support to promisers of security whose promises have no relation to the economic capacity of the country at the present time. Depression losses of jobs in the Lake cities have led millions of workers to give ear to the radio priest. The economic degradation of a generations-old agricultural depression led millions of southern poor whites to rally around Long and respond to the share-the-wealth appeal of Gerald Smith.

Each of these groups, through the "clubs" which it has founded, has taken the first steps towards party organization. The Cleveland meeting of their leaders was perhaps not much more successful than their previous effort at union at Des Moines. Jurisdictional disputes seem difficult to avoid even within the elastic frontiers of Utopia. But the recurrent attraction of these irresponsible bodies is a portent of the cohesiveness which might be imparted to them by a mutually recognized leader. Increasing adherence of American citizens to their ranks would falsify the underlying assumptions of democracy.

The recently signified irresponsibility of many of those who have too little is paralleled by the recently signified irresponsibility of many of those who have too much. The followings of the Liberty League and other less publicized committees of big business are making demands on the economic process that are no more related to reality than the demands of those who would share the wealth. The possessing irresponsibles are a greater current threat to the democratic process than the dispossessed irresponsibles because they have passed the stage of groping for political organization. The formation of the Liberty League and its like was a current development, comparable to the formation of a New Deal emergency agency, in an organizational structure whose old deal lobby was highly developed a generation and more ago. The members of this group, in the course of the last three generations, have been the makers of the unwritten constitution by which much of the recent American economic life has been regulated, the unwritten constitution whose struggle with the written Constitution is now being recorded in the decisions of the Supreme Court. Increasing adherence of American citizens to their ranks would likewise falsify the underlying assumptions of democracy.

What of the middle group? What of the political

yeomanry on whose independence a continued American democracy must rely?

Under the New Deal, the political yeomanry has taken considerable part in administration. The national policies inaugurated by the Roosevelt administration, alike in industry and agriculture, early brought into relief the local variations that characterize our continent. In a number of cases the necessity for devolution of administration has been recognized by the President.

Experience under the agricultural program is longer than under the others: in those areas where the democratic process was tried, the work done by locally elected volunteer committees has been such as to justify the method. As time has gone on, moreover, work in formulating the content of successive programs has paralleled administrative functions previously performed.

To judge the quality of the democratic process under the New Deal, however, it is necessary to look at private provisions for the expression of initiative as well as those governmentally encouraged. In the absence of private activities, the tendency would be for the executive, through its administrative branches, to arrange the generation of its own mandate. This would be pseudo-democracy. Where the government has to recruit interest in the problems of government, liberty is on the wane, and on the wane less because the government is assuming new functions than because the citizens are not exercising old ones.

The years of the New Deal, however, have given demonstrable evidence of private democratic initiative.

Revival of local interest in finding the facts on national policy, and revival of discussion of alternative methods of treating facts once found characterize important minorities of rank and file citizens up and down the country. Forums, radio forums, discussion groups, use of the mass of popularly written pamphlets on economic and social subjects which has made its appearance in the last few years, all reflect a popular concern for the state of the nation that characterized the last quarter of the eighteenth century and the middle years of the nineteenth century, but has been almost unknown in America for the past three generations.

The purpose of some of these discussion groups is self-education of their members. The purpose of others is to follow a period of self-education by a period of action, to reach conclusions, embody them in proposals for local or national policy, and work towards their formal acceptance and declaration by the appropriate legislative body.

One straw which shows the extent to which winds of doctrine are stirring the country is the mail received by public officials in Washington. Executive officers and congressmen have long been used to piles of letters and wires, stacked on their desk by pressure groups demanding support of this or that piece of legislation. But the New Deal policies have brought in a new type of communication. In a stream which each

LIBERTY UNDER THE NEW DEAL 91

of the important Court decisions has augmented to a torrent, advice on the state of the nation has come pouring in from the citizens thereof. Radio addresses have received scores of written replies. John and Jane Doe have been doing some thinking.

The combination of the policy-making groups of private citizens and the larger groups of private citizens to whom discussion of public policies has recently come to be of growing concern, offers a new political resource. Increasing adherence of American citizens to their ranks would validate the underlying assumptions of democracy.

The establishment of local constituencies made up of citizens who can contribute such quality to political life would validate the democratic process by undergirding the pyramid of representative government with a new type of support. They would validate it by supporting the present representatives in the various legislative bodies who are capable of fulfilling the legislature's constitutional mandate to formulate policy, and by replacing the present representatives who are in legislatures for other purposes. They would break the near-monopoly of policy-making recently exercised by presidential advisers. For those of their members who go on into the conduct of federal affairs, they would provide a local training ground where principles of sound administration could be learned on a less-than-continental scale, and a point of reference giving pertinence to plans.

First steps have recently taken over considerable

areas toward giving democracy a local habitation. The course of the movement during the next few years will determine American democratic destiny. The race is on between the national development of a political process and the national development of a political machine. The attitude of the administration will be one determinant in the outcome. The other will be the attitude of the people.

CHAPTER
EIGHT

———————— * ————————

A BILL

OF

PARTICULARS

THE NEW DEAL HAS BEEN RESPONSIBLE FOR RAISING high hopes among millions of people. That is a very dangerous thing to do unless these hopes can be realized. It is particularly dangerous during a period of social transition when the old landmarks are disappearing and uncertainty fills the air. In such a time the people are hungry for assurance and they are quick to follow anyone whose leadership promises the assurance they crave. But they are even quicker to repudiate leadership which promised what it could not give. And the violence of their repudiation will be in proportion to the size of the span between hopes raised and hopes fulfilled. If that span is too great the people will not only reject the leader. They will also reject the system of government and the order of society which he claimed to represent. Revolutions are not created by hopeless men. They are created by men who have had great hopes but who have been unable to realize them. Frustration and disillusion compose the soil out of which revolution inevitably grows.

If the New Deal continues for another four years it will meet its supreme test. New Deal leadership has obviously erred in promising much more than it could reasonably deliver. That is a weakness common to all political parties. But can the New Deal deliver enough to provide at least a partial sense of fulfilment? Can it even deliver enough to prevent the people from turning in fury upon its leadership and upon the democratic institutions which it presumes to serve? This is the test it will have to meet.

The purpose of this chapter is to sketch in briefest outline a national policy for the Federal Government representing the minimum program which will satisfy hopes raised by the New Deal. This minimum program is drawn up with a view to meeting the demands of liberty for a more satisfactory balance between freedom and security.

The bill of particulars under consideration is limited to the Federal Government. It assumes that state and local governments will have programs of their own and that they will supplement their own programs by participation in or coöperation with the federal program. It also assumes that responsible citizens will only wish government to do what they cannot do for themselves, and that these citizens will endeavor to solve their economic problems wherever possible through voluntary effort—either individually or collectively.

The issue of individual enterprise as over against collective enterprise has not been discussed directly in these pages. It has not been discussed because a theoretical choice between the two is both irrelevant and undesirable. As far as the United States is concerned it is highly improbable that we will ever wish to draw or be able to draw a clear dividing line between individualism and collectivism in terms of national policy. American farming will continue to be predominantly individualistic. Sections of American industry have for a long time been individualistic in their management but collectivistic in their organizational structure. It is conceivable that collective farms might be run successfully in America, but the collective farm is not likely to become the American farm pattern. On the other hand where the structure of industry is already corporate, the management cannot afford to remain individualistic. In theory it would probably be better for the nation if some of these corporate industrial structures could be broken down into individualistic units. And that may eventually be done. But the fact remains that as far as our time is concerned, some American citizens are going to operate individually and other American citizens are going to operate collectively. Hence sound national policy must make provision for development along both of these lines. National policy must also be sufficiently flexible to facilitate transition from individualistic enterprise to collectivist enterprise or vice versa when the public welfare requires transition.

ITEMS IN THE BILL

Civil Liberties

Now as always the first item in an American Bill of Particulars is an assertion of the freedom of speech and of the press and of the right of the people peaceably to assemble. The maintenance of constitutional rights is naturally a more urgent issue among those to whom these rights have been denied than among other citizens. It is doubtful whether many members of the Liberty League have ever been denied freedom of speech or have ever known what it was not to be able to assemble with their fellows. It is a different matter with large groups of industrial and agricultural workers.

The preservation of their constitutional rights to these American citizens requires action by the Federal Government. It requires action by the Federal Government because many of the forces which threaten and deny these rights operate as interstate forces and no single state possesses sufficient authority to deal with them. The recent series of incidents at Gadsden, Alabama, illustrates the situation. According to the complaint of the National Labor Relations Board, representatives of the Goodyear Tire and Rubber Company of Akron, Ohio, were responsible for inciting a Gadsden mob to the violence which cul-

A BILL OF PARTICULARS 97

minated in a brutal and inhuman assault upon members of the United Rubber Workers of America. The obvious intention of this assault was to deny to the members of the United Rubber Workers their constitutional right to freedom of speech and of assembly. Yet the states involved are not in a position to deal effectively with those responsible for this interstate assault upon constitutional liberties. The paid thugs who led the mob in one state were directed by a general staff with headquarters in another state. Alabama does not have jurisdiction over Akron, and Ohio does not have jurisdiction over Gadsden.

Such situations are made to order for the criminal elements in industry. The Lindbergh Law needs to be paralleled by a law granting the Federal Government jurisdiction over interstate interference with the free exercise of liberties guaranteed by the Constitution.

Land Legislation

It may be assumed that the Soil Conservation Program organized as a substitute for the AAA Crop Control Program will continue to be the New Deal's method of equalizing farm and industrial incomes. It is necessary to supplement the Soil Conservation Program with Federal action along two lines:

1. The extension of credit facilities in order to arrest the trend towards farm tenancy and start a trend towards individual farm ownership.

The case for such Federal action was made in a public letter addressed on May 25, 1936, by six Iowa congressmen to the President. This letter contained the following statement:

> The growing percentage of farm tenancy contains all the makings of a burning political issue; and it will remain one until the present trend does a right-about-face. Possibly you have noticed that the 1935 census shows 49.6 per cent of tenant operation in Iowa, for example, against 47.3 per cent in 1930, and 23.8 per cent in 1880. Such statistics are bound to be the yardstick by which public opinion will measure the adequacy of any farm-mortgage refinancing program.
> Heretofore no major party platform has dealt *in haec verbis* with the tenancy problem. . . . Certainly the national credit can be used successfully and entirely within constitutional limitations, to help more young men become and remain independent farm-homeowners.
> In view of our party's failure to date to enact any such legislation, and the continuing increase in the tenancy ratio notwithstanding the best efforts of the FCA, we deem it of extreme political importance that our party platform contain a definite pledge, to which we can point during the approaching campaign, that our next Administration will deal constructively with this question.

The fact that the Democratic platform makers rejected the idea of a pledge and went no further than to recognize "the gravity of the evils of farm tenancy" does not detract from the significance of the request made by the congressmen from Iowa. The situation to which they refer remains. The picture is the same for other western farm states and the picture for the South is still more sombre. This situation demands remedial action. The Bankhead-Jones

Farm Tenant Bill represents the kind of action which should be taken.

2. But the program of the Bankhead-Jones Farm Tenant Bill cannot stand alone. It needs to be supplemented by the extension of certain features of the Resettlement Administration's program, such as the retirement of submarginal land; and the organization of agricultural coöperatives in experimental centers.

The recent appropriations crisis through which Resettlement passed illustrates the precariousness of agencies not included within the budgets of regular cabinet departments.

The TVA

The Tennessee Valley Authority is serving a useful purpose both in functioning as a yardstick in the field of power production and in encouraging rural coöperative institutions leading to better standards of living in the area it covers. Similar authorities should be established in other areas.

Relation of Government to Industry

The economic security of a majority of American citizens is a product of wages and hours. The appropriateness and constitutionality of government action to alleviate, through federal relief, the insecurity contingent upon industrial unemployment have not been challenged. Both the appropriateness and the constitutionality of government action of a preventive nature, to increase the security rather than to alleviate the insecurity of industrial workers, have been challenged.

In the face of a lengthening series of decisions of the Supreme Court against industrial legislation, proposal of further legislation by the administration would appear futile. The issue is clear enough, and was never clearer than in the minimum wage decision of 1936. The New York state legislature placed a minimum wage law as a makeweight in the balance between freedom and security of women workers. With that makeweight, these workers received a weekly wage of $14.88. Without it, as indicated by evidence produced at the trial, $7.00 to $10.00 was the measure of their economic security. In the name of freedom of contract, the courts threw out the law.

Under these circumstances it would appear that the next task of the administration is to do its part in helping to clarify the public mind as to the type of relationship between government and industry required by the general welfare.

If it appears that the type of relationship required can only be established by an amendment to the Constitution, what form should an amendment take? Should it provide for congressional review and popular referendum on laws declared unconstitutional by the Supreme Court? Should it be phrased to cover specific relationships between government and industry? Or should it be a general grant of power, comparable to the enumerated powers already set

A BILL OF PARTICULARS

forth in the Constitution? Suggestions for all these types of amendment are being made.

On the other hand is an amendment to the Constitution really necessary? Are the difficulties currently felt due to governmental lack of powers under the written Constitution of 1787, or are they due to nullification by recent Supreme Court decisions of powers delegated to the Federal Government by the original Constitution? Have these recent decisions derived their definition of delegated powers from the unwritten constitution which overlaid the basic document during the latter part of the nineteenth century? Is what is really needed an amendment to the economic opinions reflected by a majority of the present justices?

The process of clarification of the public mind on major issues is always a slow one. This major issue is pressing. It is a matter on which both the administration and the people should prepare to act.

Relief and Social Security

Four different government authorities are now simultaneously engaged in dealing with the problem of unemployment and dependency. Three national agencies, the Works Progress Administration, the Social Security Board and the Resettlement Administration, each with its local representatives in the field, are paralleled by the poor law authorities of the several states.

Relief is no longer an aspect of emergency. For

years to come, the Federal Government will be engaged in administering relief.

The size of the funds currently allocated to relief by Congress, and the size of the funds provided by the tax clauses of the Social Security Act make the responsible administration of these programs of first importance alike to the recipients of future payments and to the economic stability of the nation at large.

Overlapping in some instances, incomplete coverage of need in others, and instability of policy have characterized the federal relief program to date.

A new cabinet department should be created to administer a coördinated and consistent policy. Mr. Roosevelt has served in effect as Secretary for Relief. It is not the custom of American presidents to assume cabinet portfolios. Responsible administration demands a return to cabinet government.

The basis of Federal relief policy should be cash relief according to need, with work relief provided wherever personal qualifications and local opportunities make it possible. Work relief should supplement the general program instead of constituting that program as at present.

The administration's effort to catch up the twenty-five years' lag between the United States and other countries in providing a system of social insurances is wholly praiseworthy. The present Social Security Act should, however, be revised to correct existing anomalies in coverage, to put unemployment insurance on a federal basis, to include health insurance, and to replace the present reserve basis by a pay-as-you-go system of financing.

Finance

The period of emergency finance should be officially terminated. Inflation cannot be actively checked by a government dependent on marketing its securities to feed an unbalanced budget. The reorganization of government, overdue through two administrations, should be performed, and expenditures of all departments and agencies analyzed. The current scale on which the outlay of federal funds is proceeding should be reduced, and made real to citizens of this generation by correspondingly current taxation.

Taxation

The tax policy of the United States Government is chaos worse confounded. The President's incursion into the realm of taxation in June, 1935, left the problem in general, and the mind of the country in particular, more confused than ever.

It should be obvious to even the meanest intelligence that the achievements of the New Deal cannot be paid for without a more adequate taxation program.

But no one knows what that program should be because no one has taken the trouble to collect the information regarding existing tax burdens in the states and localities without which a sound policy cannot be formulated. The President cannot afford to delay further the appointment of a commission to secure this information and make recommendations for national policy on the basis of the facts discovered. The commission should be instructed to estimate the total tax burden (both in the form of direct and indirect taxes) as this burden falls on different income groups in different parts of the country. The study undertaken by the commission would of necessity have to be a concurrent study of federal, state, county and municipal taxes.

Foreign Policy

In many respects the most notable achievement of this administration is the negotiation of the Reciprocal Tariff Agreements. It is to the credit of the United States that it should lead the way out of the morass of economic nationalism to which its policies of the nineteen-twenties made a signal contribution. But this credit is due to one man more than to the administration. The policy pursued by the Secretary of State has achieved what to other men seemed impossible. If he can crown his work by negotiating a satisfactory agreement with Great Britain, he will deserve well not only of his country but of the world.

The present state of the world makes it seem futile to talk about international coöperation in the political sphere. Yet the destiny of the United States is *with* the world and not *without* the world. We gave the League to the world. The League is dead. But a League will live again. It will live because the principle on which the League is based is the only wisdom that has yet broken into the madhouse of international relations. How long the present era of insanity will last no one knows. Wars will no doubt break out before it passes. Dictators will be destroyed and further social upheavals will occur. But the time will come when the United States will have another chance to coöperate in making the dream of Woodrow Wilson a reality. Our foreign policy should be allowed to evolve in such a way that we will be prepared when that day comes.

The above outline of national policy represents the minimum legislative program necessary to secure the blessings of liberty under the circumstances of modern life. The realization of such a program depends upon whether the democratic process of forming policy can be set to work. If that process cannot be set to work, the most ideal legislative program is worthless. In a servile state the spiritual loss is so great that no measure of material gain can compensate for it. If, on the other hand, the democratic process can be set to work, our generation too will have shared in the continuing effort "to secure the blessings of Liberty to ourselves and our Posterity."

www.ingramcontent.com/pod-product-compliance
Lightning Source LLC
Chambersburg PA
CBHW030909040526
R18240000001B/R182400PG44116CBX00005B/1